BY BRUCE W. CAMERON

POLICE CARS
A GRAPHIC HISTORY

Publications International, Ltd.

LAW and ORDER

MAGAZINE

Louis Weber, C.E.O.
Publications International, Ltd.
7373 North Cicero Avenue
Lincolnwood, Illinois 60646

Manufactured in U.S.A.

8 7 6 5 4 3 2 1

ISBN: 0-7853-2196-9

Library of Congress Catalog Card Number: 96-71797

CREDITS

PHOTOGRAPHY

The editors gratefully acknowledge the cooperation of the following people who supplied photography that helped make this book possible. They are listed below, along with the page number(s) of their photos:

Front Cover: *Law and Order* magazine.
Nicky Wright: 9, 16; **Barbara Froncza and Brandt Rosenbush, Chrysler Historical Collection:** 10, 14, 28, 34, 35, 55; **Darryl Lindsay:** 10, 12, 15, 17, 19, 21, 22, 28, 39, 40, 43, 46, 48, 49; **William J. Schintz:** 11; **Sgt. Rick Hammer:** 12; **Corporal Edwin J. Sanow:** 12, 18, 22, 25, 26, 27, 30, 31, 32, 33, 34, 35, 36, 37, 38, 40, 42, 45, 47, 48, 51, 53, 55; **Vince Manocchi:** 13, 26, 54; **Peggy Dusman, American Automobile Manufacturers Association:** 15, 18, 20, 21, 37, 38, 51, 53, 55; **Sgt. Jerry Parker:** 14; **Angie Hadrits and Chris Welch, 3M Traffic Control Division:** 17; **Tim Seaman:** 17; **Michigan State Police:** 17, 24; **Jack Markley:** 19; **Lloyd Koenig:** 20; **Sgt. James Post, Police Collectibles:** 21, 22; **Sam Griffith:** 22, 41, 203-214; **Bud Juneau:** 23; **Dan R. Erickson, Ford Photographics:** 24, 52, 54, 55, 84, 88; **Richard Quinn:** 27; **Mark Redelberger:** 39; **John Biel:** 42; **Sgt. Dave Morrison:** 43; **Pontiac Public Relations:** 43, 51; **Helen J. Earley and James R. Walkinshaw, Oldsmobile History Center:** 45; **Frank Goderre:** 46, 47; **Dave Dotson:** 52; **Darin Walsh, Chevrolet Motor Division Public Relations:** 53; **Chan Bush:** 55; **Fingermatrix, Inc.:** 118; **Doug Mitchel:** 88, 124.
All other photos provided by *Law and Order* magazine.

ARTWORK

Dan Steger, Grafix Shoppe, Eagan, MN: 193-201; **Jay Ackert and Bob Willett, Safariland, Louisville, KY:** 198; **Dick Nesbitt:** 198, 199.

OWNERS

Special thanks to the owners of the cars featured in this book for their enthusiastic cooperation. They are listed below, along with the page number(s) on which their cars appear:

Richard DeRouen, Oceanside, CA, Police Officer's Association: 9; **Debbie Colaniro:** 11; **Jerry Windle:** 16; **Sgt. Gordy Johnson and Sgt. Barry Perrou, Industry, CA:** 13; **Officer R.T. Cruz, Houston, Texas:** 20; **Chief David S. Barr, La Palma, CA:** 26; **Greg Reynolds:** 41; **Dale Shetley:** 54.

Thanks to the following for their assistance:
Commander Clarence Gross, Officer Daniel Contreras, and David J. Ciancio, Cicero Police Department, Cicero, IL; Sergeant Theodore Vernon, Jr., Illinois State Police; Lincolnwood Police Department, Lincolnwood, IL; Craig Peterson, Peterson Publications; Tom Yates.

Special thanks to Corporal Edwin J. Sanow.

CONTENTS

INTRODUCTION

The fact that Americans love their cars is a well-recognized and accepted part of our culture. Perhaps nowhere else in the world are people so mobile and tuned in to their automobiles. We love our wheels.

Automotive enthusiasts often extend their admiration to more than just cars; light trucks, heavy trucks, fire trucks, motorcycles, and even farm tractors are worshipped just as avidly by some groups. And these categories can be broken down even further, as there are enthusiasts for every subdivision—including the various vehicles acknowledged as being used by law enforcement.

There has never been a vehicle developed and manufactured specifically for general police use anywhere in the world. However, as the automobile has evolved, there have been certain models that have obtained such popular usage by law enforcement that they might be regarded by some people as being "police" cars. The most recent example is the 1991-96 Chevrolet Caprice, and before that, the 1980-89 Dodge Diplomat and (a bit later) the nearly identical Plymouth Gran Fury.

The reason there has never been a specific "police" car is very simple. Law enforcement is not a large enough market to warrant a manufacturer investing the finances needed to produce such a vehicle. The annual market for police cars in the United States is approximately 63,000 units. At the average annual production volume of 11 million cars, this represents only about one-half of one percent of the total cars produced.

This situation is not likely to change. There is such a wide diversity of need among the various law enforcement units (urban vs. rural, patrol vs. pursuit, hot climate vs. cold climate, mountain vs. prairie) that it is doubtful enough agencies would ever combine to form a large enough potential market for the vehicle of their choice. Furthermore, there is such a difference of opinion among police officers as to what qualities make a good patrol car that reaching a consensus would be nearly impossible.

We present a visible example of this difference of opinion in the greatly varying graphic designs used on police vehicles of the same make and style. What is attractive or meaningful to one police officer could be somewhat less appealing to another.

But it is this great diversity of product and opinion that makes law enforcement vehicles such an interesting subject. We have attempted to cover as wide a variety of examples as possible in order to give readers an overview of just what is encompassed by this field. For those interested in additional and more detailed information, there are a number of books and publications available for their research.

Law enforcement is universally regarded as being conservative, but the future will be exciting for police-vehicle enthusiasts, as the changes being applied today promise even more interesting and progressive developments tomorrow.

Bruce W. Cameron

Bruce W. Cameron

CHAPTER ONE

POLICE CAR HISTORY TO 1989

Historians tend to portray the early days of law enforcement as officers walking their beat while swinging a truncheon. But police have always used vehicles—in one form or another—for support functions. Horses and carriages were common in the early days, as were bicycles and motorcycles.

After the turn of the century, motorized vehicles began to appear in police fleets. One of the initial uses for trucks and large touring cars was to transport special squads of officers to trouble spots—hence the term "squad car." Early on, auto manufacturers realized the importance of this market and catered to it by building special vehicles. This practice peaked during the Prohibition era, when some were fitted with machine-gun ports, armor plating, and bullet-proof glass.

Then came the Depression, and law enforcement agencies were hit just as hard as the general public. Fleets were curtailed and vehicles purchased reflected the prevailing austerity. Ford's introduction of the potent flathead V-8 in the inexpensive 1932 Model B was a boon to police agencies working with slashed budgets.

This period also saw changes in the traditional police network. During the 1930s, state highway patrols were organized to enforce safety on the steadily expanding road systems. Meanwhile, radios (some being merely one-way) were gaining strong acceptance in metropolitan areas. Furthermore, more and more police vehicles were being identified as such, and some departments have retained vestiges of their original signage. The first red lights, which were derived from taillights, soon appeared on fenders, grilles, or rooftops.

It was during the Fifties that law enforcement fully embraced mobility. Walking beats were abandoned as communications made it possible for fewer officers driving cars to patrol greater areas and respond more quickly to service calls. It was also the beginning of the "horsepower wars" in Detroit.

In line with America's love affair with speed—and the ever-more-powerful cars the manufacturers were building to satisfy it—police cars of the Fifties were sometimes fitted with special high-performance engines not offered to civilians. This practice subsided in the Sixties, though many cruisers still carried potent big-block V-8s under their hoods. However, Detroit stopped short of offering the most powerful engines in police-package cars; either it was felt that the engines (or their adjoining drivelines) were too fragile and temperamental for the rigors of police duty, or that few agencies would be able to convince their elected officials of the need for 400-plus-horsepower patrol units.

During this period, the California Highway Patrol (which was known for putting prospective cars through extensive testing) tended to favor Dodges, Plymouths, and Chryslers, which led other departments to do likewise. While cops loved some models and hated others, Chrysler products dominated the law enforcement market for almost three decades. Not until the company discontinued its full-size rear-wheel-drive cars after 1989 did Chevrolet's Caprice and Ford's Crown Victoria take over the market.

POLICE CAR HISTORY

1

2

Previous page: This restored 1941 Plymouth wears the logo of the Oceanside, California, Police Department. This page: **1.** A 208-cubic-inch engine rated at 63 horsepower powered this 1929 Dodge paddy wagon. **2.** In its second year of operation, the California Highway Patrol used 1930 Ford coupes. **3-4.** The New York City Police Department's first radio cars were 1937 DeSotos.

3

4

1

1-2. Ford Motor Company's 1937 cars won the hearts of many law enforcement agencies. These vehicles, which cost around $700, were known for their powerful V-8 engines and overall reliability, making them the choice of many state and county highway patrol agencies as well as municipal forces. Note the red light and siren mounted on the roof of this example, as well as the red light on the front bumper; this was among the earliest installations of such equipment.

2

1

2

3

4

1

2

Opposite page: The California Highway Patrol ran some rather expensive cars in 1938. **1.** Buick's Century debuted in 1936 as something of a factory hot rod, boasting Buick's larger engine in a fairly lightweight body. This 1938 example continued that trend, making it a potent performer for the times. **2.** Another of the California Highway Patrol's vehicles was a 1938 Chrysler Imperial two-door sedan (foreground). Like the Buick Century, the Imperial was much more expensive than a contemporary Ford or Chevy, but also more powerful. **3.** This 1938 Chevrolet four-door was the car of choice of the Indiana State Police. **4.** Two-door sedans were used by many law enforcement agencies in those days, including this 1938 Ford run by the Rocky Hill, Connecticut, Police Department. *This page:* **1.** Studebaker used to produce special automobiles for police, which were highly regarded by officers. This 1938 Studebaker Commander of the Los Angeles County Sheriff's Office sports both a red spotlight and a radio antenna. **2.** The identification on the door was quite innovative for the times.

1

2

3

1. In 1939, New York City's finest patrolled in two-man teams using Plymouth coupes. **2.** The Detroit PD's Safety Education car (also a 1939 Plymouth) had an unusual public address system. **3.** Indiana's 1939 Chevrolets evidently got a lot of hard use.

POLICE CAR HISTORY

1. This 1940 Ford of the Florida Highway Patrol was quite advanced for its time, with two-tone paint and department identification across the windshield. **2.** The Lincolnwood, Illinois, Police Department had two cruisers for patrol, a 1941 Ford Super Deluxe Tudor Sedan (left) and a similar 1942 model, as well as a motorcycle. **3.** These sparkling new 1946 Ford Tudor Sedans, lined up for review, include two-way radios and an advanced-model siren/red light on their roofs, but no spotlights.

1

2

3

Opposite page: **1-2.** San Diego's finest patrolled in 1948 Fords, which were rather attractive for black-and-white squads. This car had all the modern equipment: spotlight, two-way radio, roof lights, and big siren on the fender. *This page:* **1.** This Ohio State Highway Patrol Ford was unusual in that it had an aircraft identification number on the roof. **2.** The California Highway Patrol selected Mercurys for duty in 1947. **3.** Freeport, New York, put a 1949 Chevy Styleline on patrol. **4.** The Michigan State Police added 1949 Fords to its fleet, with front- and rear-facing roof-mounted red lights.

1

2

3

4

POLICE CAR HISTORY

1

2

3

1. The 1950 Fords of the Los Angeles Police Department were easily recognized by their traditional black-and-white design. **2.** The 1950 Plymouths put on the street by the Metro-Dade Police in Miami, Florida, were unusual in their use of a green-and-white paint scheme. **3.** Ford introduced its 1950 Tudor model equipped for police service with either a special 110-horsepower V-8 engine or a 95-horsepower Six. **4.** The 1949 Chevrolets of the Indiana State Police wore a distinctive arrow-wedge graphic design.

4

1. The Pinellas Park Police Department opted for a very plain 1951 Plymouth with equally austere labeling. By this time the red light/siren on the roof was a standard fixture. **2.** The Washington State Patrol went for the 1951 Ford DeLuxe. **3.** So did the Illinois State Police; note that the paint jobs for the two are nearly identical.

1

3

POLICE CAR HISTORY

1

1. In 1952, the Houston, Texas, Police Department drove Ford Customline two-door sedans proudly marked as radio patrol. While the cars only carried a shield on the door, the two fender-mounted red lights provided police identity. 2. Unlike today's cars, the Houston cars had only the simple siren and radio control heads, leaving plenty of room inside. 3. Zanesville, Ohio's plain white 1953 Ford Mainline was assigned traffic safety duty. That was likely the reason for the public address speaker mounted on the roof. 4. The Nevada Highway Patrol copied several other states with plain black-and-white graphics for its 1953 V-8 Fords.

3

2

4

1. The Florida Highway Patrol put 1953 Pontiacs on patrol. Police were starting to identify their vehicles more, as evidenced by the lettering above the windshield. **2.** The Sacramento, California, Police Department bucked the black-and-white paint scheme commonly used throughout the state—its 1954 Fords were solid black. **3.** The Grants Pass, Oregon, Police Department installed one of the first mobile radar units on its 1954 Ford. The large siren on the right fender was impressive, but the car had no spotlights. **4.** The Highway Patrol Division of the Texas Department of Public Safety used Ford's 1954 Interceptor Police Car. The vehicle had a specially developed 160-horsepower, overhead-valve, Y-block V-8 engine capable of pushing the car to over 100 mph. Its acceleration was 20% improved over 1953 models. While highway units were still mainly two-door sedans, municipal police departments were beginning to use more four-doors.

1

2

3

4

1. This fully restored 1955 Chevrolet 150 four-door sedan is representative of the vehicles many departments used for patrol. Note the police sign in the middle of the hood. **2.** This 1955 Chevy 210, also restored, was a step up in luxury and not typical of most police vehicles. **3.** The Idaho State Police put their 1955 Chevys to work in all weather. A version of the graphic design used on this car, which was very radical for its time, is still in use. **4.** The label "plain-Jane" applies to this 1956 Ford of the Auburn, California, Police Department. It had no red lights and no spotlight—only a plain sign on the door.

1

4

3

1-3. The California Highway Patrol has used many Buicks during its history. These 1955 Centurys were specially built for the CHP. Aft of the firewall, they sported two-door sedan bodies from the lower-line Special series (all other Century two-doors were hardtops) mated to conventional Century front-ends.
4. The two-way radio was simple—just press the button to talk.

POLICE CAR HISTORY

1. The Indiana State Police got a lot of free publicity from the Chrysler Corporation by choosing the 1956 Dodge Coronet 230 as a patrol car. It was the first Chrysler vehicle made specially for police use. Touted as the "most powerful police car on the roads," this model included heavy-duty parts developed for racing. Five different engines were available. 2. The Michigan State Police put this four-wheel-drive 1956 Jeep Wagon into service, most likely in the Upper Peninsula, where it could navigate that area's deep snows. 3. West Virginia State Troopers pose with a fleet of 1956 Fords in front of the Greenbrier Hotel in White Sulphur Springs, West Virginia. The specially painted cars were used to transport dignitaries attending the Southern Governor's Conference. 4. In 1956, over 70% of all state and highway patrol cars were Fords. While the standard 215-bhp engine outperformed Chevy's police version, Ford also offered a 225-bhp version of the Interceptor V-8.

1. This 1957 Military Police Chevrolet 150 is powered by a 140-bhp, 235-cid Blue Flame Six. Chevy's newly introduced Turboglide transmission was available for the first time in a police car, but this car, being a low-cost military vehicle, had only the traditional three-speed manual. **2.** This finely restored '57 Chevy 150 is from the Department of Police Services, Shelton, Connecticut. Chevy lost the horsepower race this model year to both Ford, which offered an engine rated at 245 bhp, and Plymouth, which had an engine rated at 290 bhp.

1

2

1

2

1

Opposite page: **1.** This restored 1957 Ford of the De Soto, Kansas, Police has the big "Growler" type siren that almost over-balanced the car. That year Ford police cars could have the "Thunderbird Special" engine, rated at 245 bhp. **2.** The LaPalma, California, Police Department outfitted this sharp 1957 GMC 250 Series Panel truck. This page: **1.** The Houston, Texas, Police patrolled in 1957 Plymouth Savoy police cars, the first year Plymouth had a special police vehicle that competed with Dodge. This car had Chrysler's new "Torsion-Aire" ride for superior handling. The standard engine was the Powerflow Six, a 132-bhp, 230-cid, inline one-barrel Six, which was advertised as "the most economical six-cylinder engine on the road." **2.** Built in South Bend, Indiana, this 1957 Studebaker Parkview two-door station wagon also patrolled that city's streets.

2

POLICE CAR HISTORY

1. The Missouri Highway Patrol favored Dodges in this period. Here Patrol officials accept the latest 1958 Dodge Coronet from Dodge executives. **2.** This 1958 Dodge Coronet, although fully marked as a California Highway Patrol vehicle, was really an experimental car used to determine its suitability for their fleet. **3.** The CHP put '59 Dodges on the road in late 1958. They specified a two-door sedan with not less than a 122-inch wheelbase, weighing at least 3,800 lbs, with automatic transmission and an overhead valve V-8 with at least 350 cid and a 10.0:1 compression ratio. Also required were a calibrated speedometer, seat belts, a heavy-duty alternator, six-ply tires on 15-inch wheels, and a heavy-duty suspension.

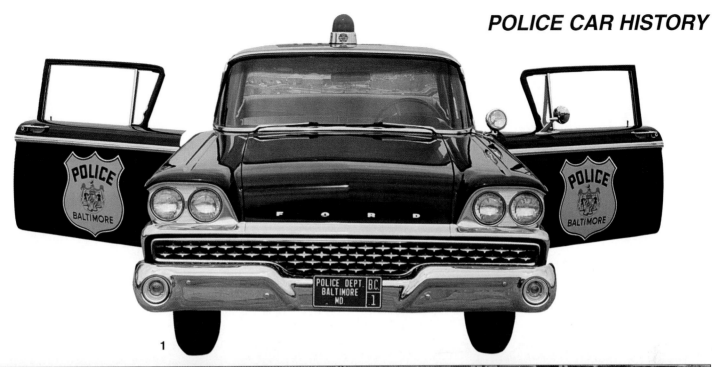

1

2

3

1-3. This 1959 Ford Custom 300 Tudor was restored by the Baltimore Police Department as a public relations project. Ford offered two police-package vehicles for '59: Custom and Fairlane. Engine choices included 292, 332, and 352 V-8s and the 223-cid Six. The Police Interceptor 352 was rated at 300 bhp. Both models had the same 118-inch wheelbase and Ford's new "Equa-Lock" differential.

1

This page: **1.** This nicely restored 1960 Chevrolet was originally from Clinton County, Indiana. Chevrolet's original offerings for police were based upon the low-end Biscayne and Biscayne Fleetmaster. There were eight powerplants offered, ranging from the 135-bhp Hi-Thrift Six to a 335-bhp, 348-cid, tri-carb V-8. **2.** Another nicely restored car is this Washington, D.C., Metropolitan Police Department 1960 Plymouth. In 1960, Chrysler cars switched from body-on-frame construction to the Unibody chassis, and the 225-cid Slant Six was introduced for police specials. *Opposite page:* **1.** Chevrolet's 1961 Biscayne sedan was that year's choice for the Iowa Highway Patrol. Biscaynes offered for police use were available with five transmissions, including Powerglide and Turboglide automatics. **2.** Ford's police entry for 1961 was based on the Fairlane. This was the first appearance of the 390-cid engine that was available in 330-bhp Interceptor and 300-bhp Thunderbird versions.

2

1

2

1

This page: **1-2.** For 1961, Dodge made a special car to meet the specs of the California Highway Patrol, and it was available only to them. This Polara had a 122-inch wheelbase and was powered by a 325-bhp, 383-cid wedgehead V-8 with a police-calibrated Carter four-barrel carburetor. It had extra leafs in the rear springs and ran on oversize 8.20×15 tires. *Opposite page:* **1.** Dodge's official police car for 1961, shown here in Michigan State Police colors, was the Dart Seneca. In 1961, more than half of the state police and highway patrol agencies in this country used cars built by Dodge. The top police engine for the Dart was the D-500 with Ram Induction, producing 330 bhp. **2.** The Michigan Sate Police also put 1961 Plymouths on the road.

2

1

2

1

2

3

POLICE CAR HISTORY

Opposite page: **1.** Dual quad carburetors were first introduced in Chevrolet police cars in 1962. There were two new engines: a 327-cid small-block V-8 and a 409-cid big-block V-8. The latter produced over 400 bhp. **2-3.** For 1962, the Dodge Dart was reduced to a 116-inch wheelbase, and the largest engine available was the 305-bhp, 361-cid V-8. The standard engine was the 101-bhp Slant Six. *This page:* **1.** Chrysler Corporation fielded its biggest police car in 1962 with the Chrysler Enforcer, shown here being introduced to the California Highway Patrol. The CHP ordered 362 of them to patrol its 82,000 miles of highways. **2.** In 1962, Ford introduced its mid-size, 115-inch wheelbase Fairlane as a police car, but its standard entry was the full-size Galaxie, shown here with Dallas Police Department markings. A four-speed manual transmission was available for the first time with its two larger engines.

1

2

1

2

Opposite page: **1.** The 1962 Plymouth Savoy was well accepted by police departments around the country. **2.** In 1963, Ford's full-size Galaxie, shown here, was more popular with police than the mid-size Fairlane. *This page:* **1.** The Chicago Police Department put a lot of these police-package 1963 Plymouth Savoy Slant Six cars on its streets. **2.** In 1963, Dodges were still preferred by the California Highway Patrol, but the emphasis was shifting in favor of fuel economy. **3.** In 1963, Studebaker offered the Lark Police Marshal with its Avanti Jet-Thrust engine.

1

2

3

1

This page: **1.** This 1964 Ford Custom used by the Franklin, Michigan, Police Department was typical of the police cars of that era. **2.** Ford's top police car for 1964 was the Galaxie model with a 330-bhp Interceptor engine. **3.** The Vermilion County, Illinois, Sheriff's Office patrolled in 1964 Chevrolet Bel Airs fitted with small-block V-8s. Note the newly introduced radar unit in the back window. *Opposite page:* **1.** 1964 was the last year for the Chrysler Newport-based Enforcer, shown here with the Missouri State Highway Patrol. **2.** The Indiana State Police was one of the many agencies using the 1964 Plymouth Savoy. **3.** In 1965, Dodge improved its Polara police car with a special handling package demanded by the California Highway Patrol.

2

3

1

2

3

1

2

This page: **1.** In 1965, Ford continued to offer two police-car models: the Custom, shown here, and the mid-size Fairlane. **2.** The Greenwich, Connecticut, Police put the 1965 Plymouth Belvedere to use on its roads. **3.** Fire departments used police specials also, such as this 1965 Plymouth Belvedere from the Colma, California, Fire Department. *Opposite page:* **1.** The 1966 Chevy Bel Air was a welcome addition to the Chicago Police Department fleet.

3

POLICE CAR HISTORY

This page: **1.** The Chicago Police Department added the 1966 Ford Custom to its extensive fleet. **2.** In 1966, the Nebraska Safety Patrol added this two-door Plymouth Fury I to its operations. *Opposite page:* **1.** Pontiac entered the police competition with its big 1967 Catalina sedan, but it was never very popular with police. **2.** The 1967 Dodge Polara, this one for the Indiana State Police, sported the 440 Magnum engine. **3.** Not to be outdone, the 1967 Plymouth Fury I, shown here in the uniform of the Michigan State Police, also had the powerful 440-cid V-8 engine, known at Plymouth as the Super Commando. **4.** In 1967, the California Highway Patrol again included Oldsmobiles in its fleet, this time the Oldsmobile Delmont 88. **5.** This 1968 Dodge Polara for the California Highway Patrol had the familiar red lights on the top. These Polaras could catch almost anything on the road at that time.

1

2

1

2

3

4

5

1

2

3

This page: **1.** The California Highway Patrol continued to use the Dodge Polara in 1969, partly due to its powerful 440-cid 4-barrel engine. **2.** Even the mid-size 1969 Dodge Coronet had plenty of interior room for police use. **3.** The 1969 Dodge Polara, along with its teammate the Plymouth Fury I, were regarded as the fastest police cars of the time. *Opposite page:* **1-2.** Oldsmobile continued to offer its Delta 88 to police in 1969. This one for the Ingham County, Michigan, Sheriff had the newly popular dual rotating lights on a roof rack. **3.** According to police auto historian Ed Sanow, the 1969 Plymouth Belvedere was one of the most popular of all Chrysler-product police cars.

1

2

3

POLICE CAR HISTORY

1

2

3

1. The Half Moon Bay, California, Police Department outfitted this marked 1972 Dodge Polara with a rooftop lightbar that included three red lights and a speaker, plus push bars, dual spotlights, and a cage in the rear seat area. **2.** This 1973 Plymouth Fury I for the New York State Police carried very plain markings. **3.** With its dual spotlights and traditional hood-mounted stop signs, this 1973 Plymouth Fury I from the Michigan State Police was clearly a police vehicle. **4.** The Sunnyvale, California, Police Department put the newly introduced, fully covered lightbars onto its full-size, four-door 1974 Chevrolet Bel Airs.

4

1

2

1. This Mount Prospect, Illinois, Police Department's 1974 Dodge Monaco carries traditional period markings. This unit is powered by Chrysler's 360-cid V-8, which was the standard engine for that model. **2.** This 1974 Dodge Monaco for the New York State Police is gaudy compared to the plain-Jane car next to it. Police car graphics were beginning to change to more clearly identify the vehicles as belonging to law enforcement agencies, but this blue-and-yellow treatment never caught on with other departments. **3.** The bold red stripe on this 1974 Plymouth Satellite for the Lawton, Oklahoma, Police Department was another unusual use of color for a police vehicle at the time. This mid-size patrol car was powered by a 360-cid V-8.

3

1

2

1

Opposite page: **1.** The Michigan State Police added the 1975 Plymouth Gran Fury to its fleet; these were the last cars able to use regular gas. This car was built on the full-size 121.5-inch wheelbase. Plymouth sold more police cars that year than any other manufacturer. **2.** The 1976 Plymouth Gran Fury joined the fleet of the Ohio State Highway Patrol. By that time, most departments had changed over to the fully enclosed lightbars. This page: **1.** Perhaps Chevrolet's best-loved police vehicle, to which this author can attest, was the 1976 Nova 9C1. This car, being mid-size, was ideal for city patrol. It was very responsive, easy to handle, and adequately powered by Chevy's 350-cid V-8. **2.** The California Highway Patrol continued to use Chrysler products, evidenced by this 1976 Dodge Coronet. It also continued to use its familiar graphics: a black car with the agency's symbol on a white door. Many of its cars were equipped with push bars.

2

1

2

3

Opposite page: **1.** In 1976, Plymouth introduced a Valiant police car to meet the demand for a more compact cruiser. Due to its light weight and brawny V-8 engine, it was among the fastest patrol cars on the road. **2.** The 1977 Royal Monaco by Dodge was popular with both city and highway agencies. *This page:* **1.** Pontiac tried again to enter the market in 1977 with its LeMans Enforcer, but again enjoyed little success. **2.** Although it got fantastic gas mileage, the 1978 Volkswagen Rabbit used in Greensboro, North Carolina, never caught on as a police vehicle. **3.** The Nevada Highway Patrol used Plymouths, including this 1978 Fury. **4.** The Minnesota State Patrol was also among those that used the 1978 Plymouth Fury.

4

1

2

Opposite page: **1.** The 1978 Ford Fairmont gained a police package at mid-year. It was offered only in the four-door version, following the nationwide trend toward better accessibility to a car's interior for transporting prisoners. **2.** The Tennessee Highway Patrol stayed with the big cars, opting for Chrysler's 1979 Newport. The blue lightbar was also the beginning of a trend. *This page:* **1.** The 1979 Chrysler Newport took top honors at the annual evaluation trials of the Michigan State Police for manufacturer-proposed police-package cars. **2.** Chevrolet's 1979 Malibu police car was touted as a replacement for the popular Nova 9C1. While it was "roomy and agile" as promoted, it never gained the acceptance of its predecessor. **3.** In 1979, the Glasgow, Montana, Police put a four-door Pontiac Catalina on its wide-open roads. **4-5.** In 1980, both the Illinois State Police and its neighbor, the Indiana State Police, chose the Dodge St. Regis for patrol duty.

1

2

3

4

5

POLICE CAR HISTORY

1. The California Highway Patrol joined with many other highway agencies in putting the 1980 Dodge St. Regis on its roads. But it was powered by a feeble 155-bhp, 318-cid, 4-barrel engine that caused CHP officers much embarrassment in high-speed chases. **2.** Also joining the crowd that assigned the 1980 Dodge St. Regis to their fleets was the Michigan State Police. The MSP retained the familiar roof-mounted, single dome, rotating red light. **3.** The 1986 Chevrolet Caprice, shown here as a Los Angeles County Sheriff's car, was the choice of many agencies in the latter part of the 1980's. **4.** Ford was still in the police car business during that decade but its cars were undistinguished in performance. Shown here is the 1981 Fairmont. **5.** The big car for Ford in 1981 was the LTD. But this car did not compare well with the other police offerings of the period.

1

2

3

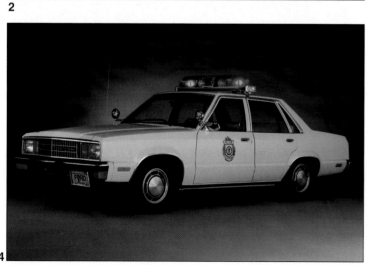

4

5

1

2

1. Florida adopted 1986 Ford 5.0-liter Mustangs for the patrol-pursuit duties of its Highway Patrol, just one of the many states following California's lead. 2. The California Highway Patrol demanded a fast pursuit vehicle in 1982, and Ford responded with its 157-bhp, 302-cid V-8 mounted in a plain Mustang coupe fitted with GT suspension and steering. Top speed was nearly 130 mph. 3. The 1986 Dodge Diplomat was the last Mopar car to be entered in the highly regarded Michigan State Police Car Evaluations. 4. In 1987, Dodge attempted to get back into the police pursuit business with its Daytona Shelby Z. The West Virginia State Police assigned one of the test cars to patrol duties and found it impressive in performance, but not very driver-friendly. 5. The Sheriff's Office of San Miguel County, Colorado, once used the four-wheel-drive 1987 Volkswagen Vanagon Syncro for its snow country patrols.

3

4

5

CHAPTER TWO

D.A.R.E. VEHICLES

Police vehicles are generally restricted to whatever the executives of the agency feel are proper—which is very often based on what the local community will accept. As a result, patrol cars are usually staid sedans sporting rather conservatives graphics, but a new breed of vehicle has come along that dares to be different.

In the late 1980s, the Los Angeles Police Department started the Drug Awareness and Resistance Education program (D.A.R.E.) to appeal to children and young adults from elementary school up through high school. It has since been adopted by numerous communities throughout the United States and even overseas. As a further tribute to its effectiveness, D.A.R.E. has been credited with being the most successful anti-drug program ever created.

D.A.R.E., which is licensed by the Los Angeles Police Department, is operated by law enforcement agencies ranging from local police departments with just one or two officers to large state agencies. The basic concept is that when individual officers gain the confidence and friendship of students by participating in their regular school activities, they are better able to impart a lesson on the dangers of drugs and how to resist their appeal.

Officers quickly learned that a sure-fire way to gain the attention of even highly suspicious and distrusting students was through their fascination with cars. Even elementary school students were charmed by specially equipped vehicles. In the early days of the program, several departments gained success by outfitting small cars such as Volkswagen Beetles with special effects. Some of these were quite elaborate, including remotely controlled blinking lights and concealed speakers that gave the impression that the vehicle was responding to questions from the audience.

It didn't take D.A.R.E. officers long to discover that hot rods, muscle cars, and dragsters held a similar attraction for the older students. Since many law enforcement officers had an interest in these cars anyway, it was a natural marriage. Only a few departments already sponsored such vehicles for other reasons, but as word of their success spread, many D.A.R.E. officers gathered their wrenches and paintbrushes and went to work on their own cars. One police agency in a rural area even customized a farm tractor.

In recent years, due to the laws allowing law enforcement to seize property belonging to drug dealers that was used in the commission of a crime, a host of unusual vehicles has been added to D.A.R.E. fleets. In many cases, they are identified as having been seized from drug dealers, providing a very effective message for youngsters.

Not every law enforcement agency has added an unusual D.A.R.E. vehicle to its fleet, however. The majority simply announce their participation in the program with the addition of the copyrighted D.A.R.E. emblem to their standard patrol cars.

D.A.R.E. VEHICLES

Previous page: The Pima County Sheriff's Department in Tucson, Arizona, dressed up a Chevy Suburban with splashy D.A.R.E. graphics. *This page:* There are no standard D.A.R.E. vehicles; they come in all shapes, sizes, and varieties. A common practice of police departments everywhere is to outfit a particularly spectacular vehicle that was confiscated as a result of a drug enforcement program. Such vehicles serve two purposes: They attract the attention of young adults, and they drive home the point that drug dealers *do* get caught and *do* pay a price. **1.** The BMW convertible at right was seized by a task force of the federal Drug Enforcement Agency and the Newport News, Virginia, Police Department. **2.** The Wallingboro, New Jersey, Police Department enlisted local businesses to help it convert this confiscated Buick Grand National into an effective teaching tool.

1

2

D.A.R.E. VEHICLES

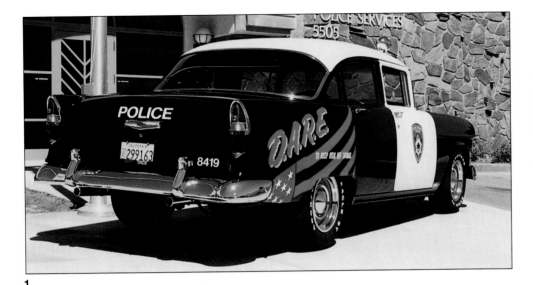

Chevrolets from the 1955-57 era are particularly popular with car enthusiasts and attract juveniles as well, especially when outfitted as D.A.R.E. vehicles. **1.** This 1955 Chevy was donated to the Atascadero, California, Police Department by a local firm. The chassis, suspension, and running gear are from an '87 Caprice patrol car. With its Flowmaster exhaust system, the high-performance 350-cubic-inch V-8 makes sweet sounds in the hot rod tradition. **2.** Halfway across the country, in the north woods of Eagle River, Wisconsin, the Vilas County Sheriff's Department transformed a classic '57 Chevy coupe into a D.A.R.E. vehicle.

1

2

D.A.R.E. VEHICLES

1

1-2. A '67 Chevelle SS 396 amply fits the bill as an exciting D.A.R.E. vehicle. The Maumee Police Department of Maumee, Ohio, made sure, by the notation on the trunk lid, that students knew the car was seized as a result of a drug investigation.
3. One of the most popular cars for D.A.R.E. programs is the Camaro. This circa-1980 example has been outfitted by the Craven County Sheriff's Office in New Bern, North Carolina. In spite of the emergency lightbars often mounted on D.A.R.E. vehicles, few of the machines ever see regular patrol duty.

2

3

1

2

3

1-3. Programs aimed at young adults often include trucks, as evidenced by the Chevy pickup of the Midwest City, Oklahoma, Police Department. **4.** Though the graphics aren't very splashy, they probably don't need to be; the Suffern, New York, Police Department's D.A.R.E. vehicle is, after all, a Corvette.

4

D.A.R.E. VEHICLES

1

2

1-2. To illustrate the show quality of its D.A.R.E. Corvette, the Loves Park, Illinois, Police Department even went so far as to identify the air filter in the engine compartment. Note the red and blue headlights and the personalized license plate. **3.** The Castle Rock, Colorado, Police Department's Camaro is part of the unit's Community Relations program as well as its D.A.R.E. program. A Vision lightbar tops off the equipment.

3

D.A.R.E. VEHICLES

1. Bright, eye-catching colors are notable decorations on the Camaro used by the Stratford, Connecticut, Police Department.
2. Another "decoration" is the anti-drug message carried on its hood. **3.** Not much question as to the purpose of this Camaro, which is tended to by the Laclede County Sheriff's Department in Lebanon, Missouri.

2

1

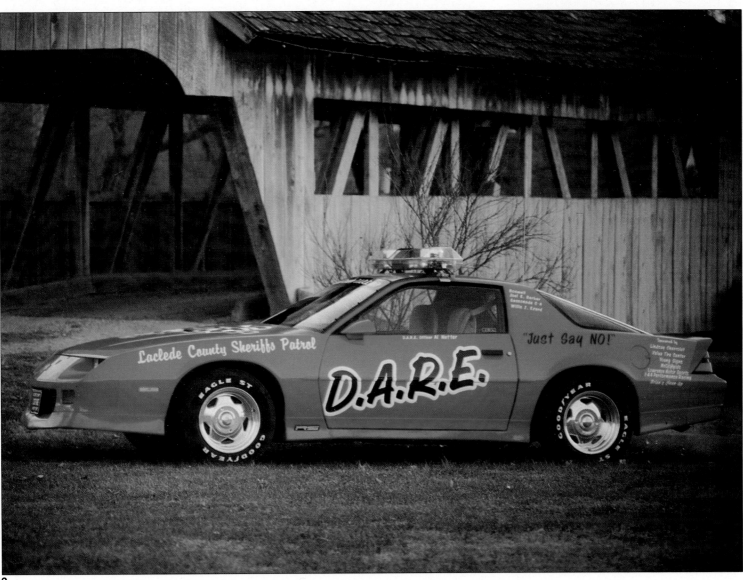

3

D.A.R.E. VEHICLES

1

2

1-3. While colorful graphics are a staple of D.A.R.E. cars, most would appear subdued compared to this 1988 Camaro, the pride and joy of the Division of Police, Department of Public Safety for the Township of Medford, New Jersey. The detailed artwork extends from the front to the sides and even includes the rear bumper. While the car carries the agency's shield on the door, the red lightbar and D.A.R.E. license plate leave no doubt as to its intended purpose.

3

1

2

3

4

1. It's unlikely many miscreants could outrun *this* black-and-white, but, of course, the Camaro dragster isn't used for patrol duty. Some police departments enlist the help of local businesses to outfit their D.A.R.E. vehicles, and it seems only fair to give them credit. **2.** Red Camaros seem to be a favorite among drug dealers, and—quite conveniently—make interesting D.A.R.E. Vehicles. **3.** The Rensselaer, New York, Police Department simply modified one of its regular Caprice sedans into an effective D.A.R.E. vehicle. **4.** Can't accuse the Pemberton Township Police of being too subtle with this D.A.R.E. Caprice. Designed by a high-school student, it is assigned to street patrol when necessary.

D.A.R.E. VEHICLES

1

2

3

1. Sometimes money doesn't appear to be an issue when developing a D.A.R.E. vehicle—as evidenced by the Caprice used by the Tallmadge, Ohio, Police Department for its anti-drug program. Fitted in full drag racing regalia, including a supercharged engine and a "tubbed" body hiding huge slicks, this car is sure to impress school kids of any age. **2-3.** The Nebraska City, Nebraska, Police Department spruced up a regular Chevrolet Astro Van for its D.A.R.E. vehicle. The listing of contributors on the rear doors includes a church, the local Jaycee's, two auto repair shops, and the telephone company. **4.** According to the message painted on the side of this sharp-looking Corvette, the Sheriff of Harris County, Texas, has placed this confiscated car into public service. A local Chevy dealer contributed the fancy paint job.

4

1

2

3

4

1-2. The Vision lightbar mount on this performance-modified Greenwood Corvette is unique, while script on the rear identifies the source of the "donated" 'Vette.
3-4. Graphics on this Portland, Texas, Police Department Caprice make it stand out from the patrol-car crowd. **5.** The Novi, Michigan, Police Department makes good use of this Chevy Lumina minivan.

5

D.A.R.E. VEHICLES

1

2

1. Though perhaps not the typical D.A.R.E. Vehicle, a Chevy Suburban can fit the bill when outfitted and designed like this one from the Pima County Sheriff's Department in Tucson, Arizona. Sheriff Dupnik didn't skimp on the budget when he added a chrome grill guard and Vision lightbar. **2.** An unusual blue-and-white paint job helps identify this Camaro as a D.A.R.E. vehicle from the New Rochelle, New York, Police Department. *Opposite page:* **1-2.** Warren County, Kentucky, Sheriff "Peanuts" Gaines, in the driver's seat, developed the patriotic graphics for this "Crimestopper Camaro." The stylized flag wraps around the car and includes 23-carat gold inlays. A message on the hood completes the work. **3.** The Grants, New Mexico, Police Department took an undistinguished Chevy Astro Van and personalized it with distinctive graphics.

1

2

3

D.A.R.E. VEHICLES

1. The D.A.R.E. program has reached even into the far Northeast, and this Chrysler minivan from the South Portland, Maine, Police Department has sparked interest among teenagers in the department's jurisdiction. It also recognizes the contributions made by local businesses. **2.** The graphics on this blue Dodge van from the West Chester, Pennsylvania, Police Department suggest it serves two purposes: the D.A.R.E. program and a community relations program. **3.** Not all D.A.R.E. vehicles are big American-made cars or trucks.Two law enforcement departments get good use out of this older Fiat X1/9 coupe: the Portageville Police Department and the New Madrid Sheriff's Department, both in Missouri.

1-2. Ford Mustangs are a favorite with young people, and this one, from the Hopewell Township, New Jersey, Police Department, is no doubt a winner with the kids. **3.** Sheriff Boyer of Jefferson County, Missouri, decorated his Ford Bronco with some bold stripes.

D.A.R.E. VEHICLES

1

2

3

1

2

3

Opposite page: **1-3.** The Crime Prevention Ford Aerostar of the Elizabeth City, North Carolina, Police Department is certainly an eye-catching vehicle. *This page:* **1.** Another eye-catching design, and another Ford Aerostar, is this one from the Jupiter, Florida, Police Department. **2.** Also from the Southeast (and also an Aerostar) is this D.A.R.E. vehicle from the Lancaster County Sheriff's Office in Lancaster, South Carolina. **3-4.** The message on the rear bumper, "Not your average black & white," about sums it up for this hot Mustang from the Sikeston, Missouri, Department of Public Safety. The graphics won a first place award in the D.A.R.E. category in the 1996 *Law and Order* Best Police Vehicle Design Competition.

4

D.A.R.E. VEHICLES

1

1. Pima County Sheriff Dupnik, from Tucson, Arizona, even adorns his regular patrol vehicles with D.A.R.E. identification. This attractive, police-package Ford Crown Victoria, outfitted with a cage and push bars, has a paint scheme that harmonizes with the desert county in which the vehicle regularly operates. **2.** A set of fancy wheels and some colorful lettering can do wonders for an otherwise plain sedan, as shown by this Crown Vic from the Lafayette, Indiana, Police Department. This department won a design competition one year for its radical graphics but decided they were inappropriate for the community, so it reverted back to a more modest look.

2

1-2. Another example of aftermarket wheels and fancy graphics doing an admirable job of dressing up an average car is this Crown Vic of the Wanaque, New Jersey, Police Department. **3.** A non-police-package Ford Taurus assumes D.A.R.E. responsibilities for the Commerce City, Colorado, Police Department.

D.A.R.E. VEHICLES

1

2

1-2. Not a lot of Jeep CJs are converted to D.A.R.E. vehicles, but the Livonia, Michigan, Police Department has made an exception. The popular vehicle has been dressed in colorful graphics. **3.** Another Jeep, this one a Cherokee, wears bold identification courtesy of the Cumberland County Sheriff's Office.

3

D.A.R.E. VEHICLES

1

2

1-2. "You use...you lose!" In this case, a drug dealer lost a nice Pontiac Firebird to the Plainfield, Illinois, Police Department, which promptly turned it into a striking D.A.R.E. vehicle. **3-4.** You don't see many Porsche 928s around, particularly dressed up as D.A.R.E. vehicles, but that didn't stop the Alpine City, Utah, Police Department.

3

4

D.A.R.E. VEHICLES

1

1. In the early days of the D.A.R.E. program, many departments used Volkswagens to reach the younger students. The vehicles were often rigged with remote controls for blinking lights and sound in response to posed questions. This unit from the New Britain, Connecticut, Police Department is of interest to young people because of its rarity; despite the staggering number sold, they are seldom seen on the streets today.
2. The Fort Meade, Florida, Police Department has a complete D.A.R.E. program in progress that involves students, McGruff the Crime Dog and his miniature car, and the agency's bicycle patrol.

2

1

2

1-2. This fully restored 1951 International Harvester McCormick Farmall "A Series" tractor is probably the most unusual D.A.R.E. vehicle around. It was designed to draw the attention of kids and adults while adhering to the pioneering and agricultural heritage of the city of Union Gap, Washington. The mural on the back depicts the early pioneers as they moved West with a Native American companion. A functional siren, lightbars, and a public address system were added to complete the image of a police vehicle. The tractor pulls D.A.R.E. graduates on a 16-foot trailer during civic parades.

CHAPTER THREE
MUNICIPAL POLICE CARS

In the early 1900s, agencies could order their police cars in any color they wanted—as long as it was black. It wasn't until later that the more adventurous departments experimented with white cars, some even going so far as to paint the word "Police" on the sides. Then a few creative souls used white doors on black cars . . . and the "black and white" was born.

Eventually, agencies added more sophisticated identification to their vehicles, often applying a decal of the department's badge or shield on the sides. Some even decided to abandon the now-traditional black-and-white paint scheme and to order their vehicles in various colors. These were often chosen to match the officers' uniforms; blue was most popular for municipal agencies, brown or green being the norm for Sheriff's cars.

A similar transformation was seen in police car lighting. Early vehicles commonly used colored spotlights. These were followed by red lights installed on the rooftops; first a single turret with a revolving interior light (which became known as a "gumball"), then two turrets, often mounted on a crossbar. And it didn't take suppliers long to further improve on these designs. First they added strobe lights, then additional lights such as blue lights, takedown lights, and alley lights, enclosing them all in streamlined fixtures. The latest designs feature a series of lights in wedge-shaped bars that provide better side illumination.

Through the 1950s and on into the '60s as well, a wide variety of cars were tapped for police use, ranging from six-cylinder Studebakers to Buicks with huge V-8s. And not all were four-door sedans either; two-doors were quite common, and even station wagons were seen.

By the mid-Sixties, however, most agencies were using full-size sedans, primarily Chevrolets, Fords, Dodges, or Plymouths, though AMC was represented by a fair number of Matadors and Ambassadors in the early-to-mid Seventies, after which it discontinued its full-size cars. That left the Big Three—until Chrysler Corporation killed off the Dodge Diplomat and Plymouth Fury after 1989 . . . and then there were two.

For the past several years, the Chevrolet Caprice and the Ford Crown Victoria have been the preeminent police vehicles in the United States. But with the demise of the Caprice after the '96 model year and the expected shortage of Crown Vics, that scenario will likely change. And, in some departments, it already has.

Due in part to the limited choice among domestic sedans, many police agencies have experimented with alternatives. These include sport-utility vehicles (in both two- and four-wheel drive) and a smattering of foreign makes.

That brings us to the start of this chapter. While the choice of domestic cars had dwindled over the years, by 1990 the variety of graphics had expanded somewhat. Early attempts at more imaginative paint schemes were usually drawn up by amateur artists. More recently, however, professional studios have been enlisted to devise more elaborate and artful designs.

In appreciation of (and perhaps even as a catalyst for) these efforts, *Law and Order* magazine began holding a Police Car Graphics contest in 1990. The following are examples of the fine designs that have been sent in over the last seven years and, coincidentally, a sampling of the wide range of vehicles currently in use.

MUNICIPAL POLICE CARS

1

2

3

Previous page: An older Crown Vic lights up the Minnesota night. *This page:* **1.** The Birmingham, Alabama, Police Department used a bold blue color to accentuate the gold shield on the doors of its 1993 Ford Crown Victoria police car. **2.** The Rogers, Arkansas, Police Department favored a traditional look with the basic law enforcement black-and-white colors, but added a modern touch with a flash of red and blue on the doors of its 1993 Ford Crown Victoria. **3.** Not only is the Cave Springs, Arkansas, Lincoln Continental Mark VIII unusual for a police car, but the red color overlaid with gold is also a break from tradition. The graphics show originality of design. **4.** This circa-1980 Dodge Diplomat of the Hamburg, Arkansas, Police Department has a conservative design typical of many small communities.

4

1

2

3

4

5

1. California is known for its "black-and-whites," but Cathedral City gave this 1995 Caprice a different look with blue lettering on the doors. **2.** San Clemente, California, got away from that state's traditional colors for its 1989 Caprice. **3.** Santa Monica, California, also went with the nontraditional look but reduced the width of the blue stripe on its 1994 Crown Vic. **4.** Cherry Hills, Colorado, borrowed the California black-and-white look. **5.** Aspen, Colorado, has used Saabs as police cars for the last decade.

MUNICIPAL POLICE CARS

1. Being in ski country, Breckenridge, Colorado, opted for the four-wheel-drive Ford Explorer. 2. Broomfield, Colorado, tried a different black-and-white treatment and type style on its Caprice. 3. This 1991 Caprice from Arvada, Colorado, features an unusual type style. 4. The striping and lettering on this Crown Vic from the Eaton, Colorado, Police are certainly eye-catching. 5. Police agencies in the East tend to favor darker colored cars, as evidenced by this Ford from East Haven, Connecticut.

1

2

3

4

5

1. The black-and-white paint scheme is used in New Britain, Connecticut, but script-style type imparts a modern look to the vehicle. **2-3.** Special wheels and colorful graphics impart a unique look to this 1990 Chevrolet Caprice from the Shelton, Connecticut, Police Department. Note that the police identification extends even to the lightbar. The slogan on the rear fender is also unusual. **4.** This 1990 Ford Crown Victoria for the Weston, Connecticut, Police Department is brightened by a bold, reflective, yellow stripe.

1

2

3

4

MUNICIPAL POLICE CARS

1

2

1. This Longwood, Florida, Police Mustang is assigned to Traffic Enforcement. **2.** The graphics for this 1996 Crown Victoria of the Bethany Beach, Delaware, Police won a first place award in *Law and Order*'s Best Police Car Design Competition in 1996. Judges said the unusual wave effect was especially interesting. **3.** This confiscated Mercedes is identified as a New Castle, Delaware, police car by the shield on its door. The lightbar is added emphasis.

3

1. The Panama City, Florida, Police have a traditionally marked black-and-white Caprice. **2.** This Caprice from the Plantation, Florida, Police shows originality in color, but has subdued identification. **3.** The stream of yellow on this Crown Vic from the Ponce Inlet, Florida, Police is innovative. **4.** Graphics on the St. Petersburg, Florida, police cars are complemented by the colors used.

MUNICIPAL POLICE CARS

1

2

3

4

5

6

This page: **1.** Clean but simple graphics make this Crown Vic for the Morrow, Georgia, Police very appealing. **2.** The Bellevue, Idaho, Marshal has taken the black-and-white look to its extreme with this almost sinister-looking older Caprice. **3-5.** Cicero, Illinois, police vehicles sport a new, modern graphic design, as shown on the department's Chevrolet Lumina and Jeep Cherokee. **6.** The front-seat area inside the 1995 Crown Vic looks spacious in this photo, but it feels very crowded at the end of an eight-hour shift. *Opposite page:* **1-2.** This Caprice from the Charlestown, Indiana, Police Department is an impressive example of how a modern look can be achieved along with spectacular patrol-car safety in the dark.

1

2

1

2

3

1. Even a small, one-car police department can have attractive vehicle graphics, as shown here on this Dayton, Indiana, Caprice.
2. Indianapolis displays good taste in their use of colors to decorate their fleet of Caprices. **3.** The use of strobe lights is growing because of their contribution to safety. This Merrillville, Indiana, police car shows how effective they can be. **4.** The police identification in the design of this 1996 Caprice from Whiteland, Indiana, is striking, but not easily seen. **5.** The small village of Beecher, Illinois, was innovative in the use of the state silhouette and a star to raise their ordinary black-and-white to award-winning status in the *Law and Order* competition.

4

5

1

2

3

4

1-2. The Cherry Valley, Illinois, Police Department graphics appear distinctive not only during the day, but, with the help of bold reflective materials, at night as well.
3. The Elk Grove Village, Illinois, Police Department also uses reflective materials extensively, for a very attractive appearance on its Caprices. Wrapping the stripes around the Village symbol is a nice touch.
4. The graphics on this Caprice from the Spring Grove, Illinois, Police Department wrap completely around the car—from front bumper to rear deck—for a unique design. The large lettering on the hood is also unusual.

MUNICIPAL POLICE CARS

1

2

3

4

5

6

1. The Vernon Hills, Illinois, Police brightened their dark blue car with a broken red stripe and bold, yellow lettering for the name. **2.** This dark blue car from the Waterloo, Illinois, Police Department uses a subtle, complementary-colored stripe that runs over the trunk lid. **3.** Wauconda, Illinois, graphics are a combination of different stripes, colors, and the community symbol. **4.** An attractive variation on a black-and-white paint scheme is this Caprice for the Woodstock, Illinois, Police. **5.** Police in Manchester, Iowa, go with banners of patriotic colors for their patrol vehicles. **6.** The Burlington, Iowa, Police adorned their dark Crown Vic with a bold, golden stripe.

MUNICIPAL POLICE CARS

1. The Andale, Kansas, Police Department may drive Ford Tauruses, but they outfit them rather well with equipment and graphics. Note the siren and lights mounted on the push bars. **2.** The Hutchinson, Kansas, Police Department wants to make sure that anyone following its Crown Vics is aware that they are behind a police car. The free-style banner and use of script for the town name are modern touches. **3.** It may be just a white Caprice, but the Bowling Green, Kentucky, Police Department has decorated it very nicely with a simple gold shield and blue lettering. **4.** The Brandenburg, Kentucky, Police Department went wild with a modern graphic treatment for its cars, perfectly matching Brandenburg's "City on the Move" slogan. **5.** Since there is a Toyota Camry assembly plant in Georgetown, Kentucky, politics might account for the police using Camrys as patrol cars. In any case, the simple blue-on-white paint scheme is attractive.

1

2

3

4

5

93

MUNICIPAL POLICE CARS

1

2

3

1. The Russell Springs, Kentucky, Police spruced up their white Caprice with modern graphics in two tones of blue. **2.** The special agency that patrols the Lake Pontchartrain Causeway outside of New Orleans decorated their cars with an illustration of their beat. **3.** The New Orleans Harbor Police have graphics distinct from the city police. **4.** Baltimore, Maryland, police chose a subdued design for their white Crown Vic.

4

1

2

3

4

5

6

1. The Elkton, Maryland, Police went with a splash of color to identify their Crown Vic. **2.** Over in Greenbelt, Maryland, police took a nontraditional approach by decorating their black-and-white with bold, reflective lettering. **3.** The City of Hyattsville, Maryland, kept the design of its Dodges subdued with pastel blue and white, highlighted by a small city crest. **4.** The Boston, Massachusetts, Police Department uses a type style that clearly distinguishes its cars from those of surrounding communities. **5.** Easton, Maryland, Police are sure that their cars are going to be easy to identify, with the strong yellow police wording. **6.** The Massachusetts Bay Transportation Authority doesn't have room on the side of its cars for its full name, so instead it uses the agency crest for identification.

MUNICIPAL POLICE CARS

1

2

3

1. The importance of emergency lights for the safety of patrol cars is evidenced by this night shot of a Somerset, Massachusetts, Police Department Crown Victoria with all lights ablaze. **2.** In Michigan, many of the community police agencies use vehicles that are produced locally. The Auburn Hills Police Department makes good use of this clearly marked Dodge Intrepid, even though the vehicle is not equipped with a police package. **3.** Another community with close ties to Chrysler Corporation is Blissfield, Michigan, which accounts for their use of this distinctively marked Dodge Intrepid. **4.** Dearborn, Michigan, is the home of the Ford Motor Company; therefore it stands to reason that the police department would use Ford products. The agency regularly tests new models for the company, even putting various Lincolns on patrol. **5.** With all lights flashing, this Caprice of the Delta College, Michigan, Police shows its night-safety image.

4

5

1

2

3

4

1. This dramatic nighttime photograph of a Grand Rapids, Michigan, Police Caprice shows that even a dark car can be adequately seen at night if the proper reflective materials are used. **2.** The Niles Township Police Department uses reverse lettering at the top of the windshield to help identify its cars. **3.** An unusual hood design graces this car from the Tuckerton, New Jersey, Police Department. **4.** The flow of the simple but effective graphics on this Redford Township, Michigan, Police Caprice makes good use of the car's body lines.

MUNICIPAL POLICE CARS

1

2

3

4

5

6

1. As is popular in many northern cities, the Zeeland, Michigan, Police have a brightly marked, dark car. 2. The Goodview, Minnesota, Police patrol in a sprightly police-package Chevy Lumina. 3. Minneapolis Police cars display a splash of modern graphics. 4. The Olivette, Missouri, Police decorate their cars with the community's logo. 5. This Whitefish, Montana, Police car carries simple shield-and-stripe graphics. 6. The University of Nebraska at Karney Police put a Pontiac Grand Prix on patrol.

1

2

3

1. A simple but highly effective design is used by the Keene, New Hampshire, Police Department. **2.** The Milford, New Hampshire, Police have bright graphics on a Crown Vic with an unusual two-tone treatment. **3.** A patrol car has to have an effective design visible in any kind of weather, as shown by this Caprice from the Bridgewater Township Police Department in New Jersey. **4.** Police in Clinton Township, New Jersey, enliven a standard black-and-white design with a broad band of color. **5.** The Borough of Cresskill, New Jersey, added the city crest to a wrap-around striping theme. **6.** Police in Guttenberg, New Jersey, used a subtle stripe of yellow to dress up the blue stripes and city crest on this Caprice.

4

5

6

1

2

1

2

3

4

5

Opposite page: **1-2.** These daytime and nighttime photos of a Montville Township, New Jersey, police car show how reflective materials can improve visibility and increase safety. *This page:* **1.** This Stafford Township, New Jersey, police car displays a unique interpretation of the traditional black-and-white theme. **2.** This Caprice from Petoskey, in the northern reaches of Michigan, gives the impression that it is ready for any police business that may come its way. **3.** The Wyckoff, New Jersey, Police have brightened their black-and-white car with a different placement of the accent stripe. **4.** The Las Cruces, New Mexico, Police applied interesting Native American graphics that are familiar to the area. **5.** Taos, New Mexico, Police also adapted a Native American motif on their Lumina patrol cars for a bright and lively look.

MUNICIPAL POLICE CARS

1

2

3

1. This Albany, New York, Police Department car has the right look for nighttime safety. **2.** With its extra red grill lights and bold lettering on the hood, this Batavia, New York, police car lets people know exactly who is behind them. **3.** The Fishkill, New York, Police Department applied swooping graphics and added the municipal crest for specific identification.

1

2

3

4

1. Red police vehicles are a familiar sight in New York state, and this Hyde Park Police Department car with the red top is not considered unusual in that area. **2.** The Rockville Centre, New York, Police Department added a patriotic theme to its vehicles. **3.** Special wheels were added to the Rosendale, New York, Police Department Caprice that complement the silver car and its graphics for a novel look. **4.** The Saint Regis Mohawk Tribal Police Department in Hogansburg, New York, applied an interesting graphic design to its vehicles, befitting the area's native heritage. **5.** The novel and bold graphics on this Caprice from the Watkins Glen, New York, Police Department give an appropriate impression of speed.

5

MUNICIPAL POLICE CARS

1

3

4

1-2. A very unusual graphic treatment was developed by the Asheville, North Carolina, Police Department for its patrol cars. Inside the letters are illustrations of the city's most prominent features: building architecture and mountain scenery. 3. Because of the difficult terrain within its jurisdiction, the Beech Mountain, North Carolina, Police Department uses four-wheel-drive vehicles with an interesting graphic design that refers to the community's geography. 4. This police-package Chevrolet Lumina presents a sleek look with the reflective graphics developed by the Belhaven, North Carolina, Police Department. 5. The Hendersonville, North Carolina, Police Department has a more traditional black-and-white patrol car, but added a flash of color to make it more distinctive.

5

1

2

1. The Kannapolis, North Carolina, Police added blue stripes to their white car and applied the town crest to the door. **2.** The Archbold, Ohio, Police also added stripes to a white car—in this case, a Pontiac Bonneville. **3.** The Lincoln Heights, Ohio, Police used a graphics firm to develop an attractive and professional-looking car design. **4-5.** Another variation of the traditional black-and-white patrol-car look is this one from Springfield Township, Ohio. At night, the reflective materials make a dramatic impression.

3

4

5

MUNICIPAL POLICE CARS

1

1. The Twinsburg, Ohio, Police Department is one of the few agencies using the Dodge Intrepid for patrol duties, although it does not have a police package. The attractive graphics look professionally done. **2.** This photograph of the Moore, Oklahoma, Police Department Caprice strikingly shows the effects of the emergency lights at night. **3.** The Tulsa, Oklahoma, police cars are effectively marked as police vehicles, but the Tulsa identification is subtle. **4.** While conforming to the tradition of using dark cars in the Northeast, the Pennsylvania State Capitol Police, in Harrisburg, clearly differentiate their vehicles from other local agencies. **5.** The Beaverton, Oregon, Police took a conservative but attractive approach to designing their black-and-white patrol car.

2

3

4

5

1

2

3

4

5

1. The Jones Township Police Department in Wilcox, Pennsylvania, prefers a conservative dark car. **2.** The Radnor Township Police in Wayne, Pennsylvania, brightened up their car with strong red and white stripes. **3.** Orange is unusual on police cars, but the Township of Kingston, Pennsylvania, uses it to make its cars stand out. **4.** The Citadel Police in South Carolina attractively marked their unusual dark patrol car. **5.** The Cookeville, Tennessee, Police have a different slogan on their cars.

MUNICIPAL POLICE CARS

1

2

This page: **1.** The Addison, Texas, Police Department chose a very simple design that gives a clean look to their unusual Pontiac Bonneville patrol car. Note the spoiler on the trunk. **2.** A rendition of the famous Bowie Knife is included in this unique design on the Bowie, Texas, Police Department patrol car. **3.** Here is a different design approach to the traditional black-and-white patrol car, from the Forest Hill, Texas, Police Department. **4.** The Hewitt, Texas, Police Department extended the blue stripe along the sides and over the trunk of its plain white patrol car, while blending in the familiar 911 logo. *Opposite page:* **1.** The Lake Dallas, Texas, Police use simple but effective graphics. **2.** The Laredo, Texas, Police were equally conservative on their design. **3.** It's not a police-package car, but the Nassau Bay, Texas, Police use a Chevy Celebrity for patrol duty. **4.** The only way to tell that this car is from the Richardson Bay, Texas, Police is by the stylized "R" on the rear fender. **5.** In Gunnison, Utah, you can see this Taurus coming from a long way off.

3

4

1

2

3

4

5

MUNICIPAL POLICE CARS

1

2

1. This Dodge Diplomat from the Ogden City, Utah, Police displays graphics that are typical of the old designs. **2.** The 1993 and 1963 Fords show the contrast between old and new for the Chesapeake, Virginia, Police. **3.** The Hartford, Vermont, Police chose simple graphics for this older Dodge. **4.** The Manchester, Vermont, Police went for a grey-and-black two-tone paint job but went light on the lettering. **5.** The Winooski, Vermont, Police must have bought their design from the same firm as did Hewitt, Texas (see page 108).

3

4

5

1

2

1. The thickening blue stripes coming from the lighthouse on the door are a nice design touch for the Mukilteo, Washington, police car. 2. This 1996 Taurus is not a police-package car, but the Grafton, West Virginia, Police turned it into a striking patrol car. 3. From the graphics on their patrol cars, you might get the impression that the Chenequa, Wisconsin, Police Department patrols in the deep woods. 4. The new Eagle River, Wisconsin, patrol cars have a rendering of an eagle as their focal point. 5. The old Eagle River patrol cars had a graphic treatment with the town's name done in script—also a striking design.

3

4

5

MUNICIPAL POLICE CARS

1

1. The Town Marshal of the Fredonia, Wisconsin, Police Department selected a silver-gray Caprice as a patrol car, which is set off nicely with blue-and-white graphics. 2. In Maple Bluff, Wisconsin, just outside Madison, the police adapted a standard graphic design to their black Taurus and equipped it with a Vision lightbar. 3. The Mount Horeb, Wisconsin, Police Department splashed red on its police-package Chevy Lumina for a unique look. 4. Looking like it just swept out of a television police series, this Dodge Diplomat from the Township of Ripon, Wisconsin, has the typical black-and-white look so familiar to TV viewers.

2

3

4

MUNICIPAL POLICE CARS

1. The Royal Canadian Mounted Police are no longer mounted on horses; they drive Ford Crown Victorias like other law enforcement agencies, but the tradition is carried on by the symbolic Mountie on the rear fender. **2.** The Traffic Police of the Shanghai, China, Public Security Bureau no longer scoot around town on motorcycles or in old military jeeps, as they have modernized with attractive Volkswagen sedans. **3.** It's not a police-package Crown Vic, but police officers from the Minister of Interior in the Republic of Croatia enjoy their modern Fords. **4.** This European Ford is marked for the Northumbria police force in England.

MUNICIPAL POLICE CARS

1

2

3

1. It has been suggested by the Home Secretary in England that all its Traffic Police should have a more recognizable and coordinated identity. It was suggested that this new design, called the Battenburg, be considered by all forces. It has been tried by some, but is not yet widely seen. **2.** This Jaguar, of the Warwickshire Constabulary, is in the old design of that force. **3.** This West Midlands Vauxhall Senator is also decorated in one of the old designs that is being replaced in England. **4.** The Polizei in Germany have adopted green as the dominant color on their vehicles. Their patrol cars vary with the region, and are often based upon what automobile is assembled there.

4

1

2

1. This foreign Ford carries the new colors recently selected by New Zealand police administrators in an effort to modernize the force. 2. The traffic police in the Republic of Slovenia are privileged enough to drive BMWs. 3. This police car from Madrid, Spain, belongs to the Policia Nacional. 4. Believe it or not, this is actually one of the better-looking vehicles in the Moscow police fleet.

3

4

CHAPTER FOUR

STATE AND COUNTY POLICE CARS

According to Department of Justice statistics, there are 17,120 law enforcement agencies in the United States. Of these, 3084 are county departments and 49 are state agencies—Hawaii being the only state without one.

Two agencies are widely recognized by their peers as being the leaders in vehicle testing. Each year, the Michigan State Police conduct independent tests of vehicles offered for law enforcement use. The tests include top speed runs, acceleration times, braking distances, and handling prowess. The annual trials are attended by representatives from over a hundred departments, and the agency prepares a detailed report that it distributes to any police agency that requests it.

The Los Angeles County Sheriff's office also conducts its own vehicle tests each year. While many of the tests are similar to the Michigan trials, this event is more focused on urban law enforcement requirements. Unlike the Michigan trials, the Los Angeles test results are kept confidential.

The type of vehicles an agency uses depends largely upon its responsibilities. A Sheriff's office charged only with court duties has no use for the pursuit-type vehicles required by some of its counterparts, so the officers typically drive smaller, front-wheel-drive sedans without police packages.

Being traditionally conservative organizations, state police agencies have only recently followed the trend toward more modern, contemporary graphics. There is also a move to reduce, if not eliminate, the use of unmarked highway patrol cars for two reasons: a concern over people being assaulted by criminals misrepresenting themselves as police officers in unmarked cars, and the absence of prominent emergency lights.

As the performance gulf between the typical police sedan and the sporty cars sold to the public widened in the Eighties, many state agencies adopted high-performance coupes for highway pursuit duty—even though there were serious questions as to their suitability for patrol use. With all the equipment modern highway patrol vehicles must carry today, space is tight even in full-size cars, and carrying prisoners in cramped two-doors would be awkward, if not impossible. Yet many states count on their fleets of Mustangs, Camaros, and the like to reel in speeders traveling at triple-digit velocities.

Other jurisdictions encounter extreme conditions of another sort. Where bad weather and poor roads are common, four-wheel-drive vehicles are often the norm. A long-time favorite for this type of duty—and a staple with the U.S. Border Patrol—was the Dodge Ramcharger. But since production of that vehicle ceased after 1993, other sport-utes have begun to take its place.

In fact, the profile of police vehicles in general will change dramatically in the next few years. Chevrolet has discontinued the popular Caprice, and Ford won't likely build enough Crown Victorias to take up the slack. Filling the void will likely be front-wheel-drive sedans and 2/4WD sport-utilities, as some manufacturers (notably Chevy and Chrysler) have already introduced, or announced future availability of, police packages on these vehicles.

STATE AND COUNTY POLICE CARS

1

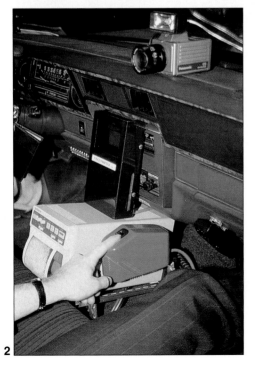

2

3

Previous page: An Illinois State Police Caprice sits in front of Buckingham Fountain in Chicago. *This page:* **1.** The California Highway Patrol (CHP) has a reputation for innovative ideas regarding mobile patrol—and putting those ideas to the test. An evaluation of this 1989 Toyota Camry showed it didn't measure up to their requirements. **2.** Shown being tested by police is an instant criminal identification system, which communicates through cellular links with databases that accept fingerprints and mug shots from the field. **3.** The CHP field-tested a new logo on some of its cars but kept the familiar star on the white door.

1

2

1. The Arapahoe County, Colorado, Sheriff's Office has an attractive symbol as part of its graphic design. Posting signs on the back bumper is different, and the reflective material on the trunk is effective. **2.** Florida Sheriffs all follow the same green-and-white color scheme on their vehicles, but each has its own design. Sarasota County has a clean, graphic look. **3.** In Fort Myers, Florida, the Lee County Port Authority has dark cars, which is unusual in the South due to problems with heat build-up. The agency's graphics stand out well.

3

STATE AND COUNTY POLICE CARS

1. The space shuttle *Endeavour* at Cape Canaveral, Florida, doesn't really blast off from the roof of a Brevard County Sheriff's Office patrol car, but it certainly makes an interesting backdrop. 2. Orange County, Florida, is the home of the globally famous Disney World and attracts hoards of tourists, so it's only proper that the Sheriff would have a nicely designed patrol vehicle. 3. By contrast, this is the undistinguished former graphic design of the Orange County patrol cars. The redesign was needed to bring the cars up to current levels of modern graphic design and safety. 4. The vehicle fleet of the Lee County, Florida, Sheriff's Office includes this Ford Aerostar van with the standard colors used by all Florida Sheriffs. 5. The Lee County design features a nicely replicated gold star of the Sheriff's Office.

1

2

3

4

5

1

2

1. Yes, it really is a State Police car! This brightly decorated Crown Vic is a member of the Indiana State Police fleet. It is assigned to help promote safe-driving programs and is scheduled to attend public events around the state. 2. The rear of the car gives credit to the organizations that contributed to the artistic look of this special vehicle. 3. This Indiana Sheriff's Caprice is typical of the colors and design of the County fleets in that state. 4. Sheriff Mecum, of Hall County, Georgia, got some strict traffic enforcement out of this Mustang designated for that effort. Note the radar head mounted in the back window.

3

4

1

2

4

3

This page: **1.** The Dewitt County, Illinois, Sheriff chose a modern, flowing design for his white Caprice. **2.** Sheriff Sam Hiller of Perry County, Illinois, is a conservative but progressive and modern-thinking peace officer, and his patrol vehicles are designed to reflect that attitude. **3.** While the state of Illinois does not require that Sheriffs follow a set color standard or design for their vehicles, they generally choose shades of brown, as did the Sheriff of Iroquois County. **4.** A red law enforcement vehicle might be considered strange in most parts of the country, but not in the Northeast, and especially not in New York state. This well designed car is from the Genesee County Sheriff's Department in Batavia, New York. *Opposite page:* **1.** Illinois does get snow, as the Illinois State Police well know. This semi-marked Caprice is decorated with the graphic design used prior to 1996.

STATE AND COUNTY POLICE CARS

1

2

1. In 1996, the Illinois State Police adopted a policy of equipping all the marked vehicles in their patrol fleet with a full complement of lights, including a lightbar. This Caprice also has the new "wedge" graphic design introduced in 1996. **2.** It is easy to see from this photo of a very neat Illinois State Police car interior why many police officers believe only a full-size sedan will accommodate them and their equipment. This one doesn't even have a computer or video camera installed. **3.** The state of Texas has more Sheriffs than any other state, and includes the Kleberg County Sheriff's Office, in Kingsville. This is the vehicle design used prior to the introduction of a new paint scheme and graphics in 1993.

3

1

2

1. A committee of members of the Flathead, Montana, Sheriff's Department selected several proposed designs for new graphics on the agency's patrol cars. The entire department then voted and selected this design. The message on the front fender is very poignant; it reads, "Professionals in Law Enforcement." **2.** Even Sheriffs' departments have the black-and-whites so familiar to law enforcement, but this one from the McPherson County, Kansas, Sheriff has been upgraded with red stripes on the doors. The mud flaps might be considered a necessity in some parts of Kansas.

STATE AND COUNTY POLICE CARS

1. In the Bluegrass state of Kentucky, the gray uniforms of the State Police troopers match the silver-blue color of their cars. The square-headed spotlight is unusual. 2. This action photograph of a Kentucky State Trooper at an actual traffic stop shows very vividly the effect of his vehicle's emergency lights. If the car had a fully equipped lightbar it would be even more visible. 3. This car, from the Sedgwick County, Kansas, Sheriff's Office, is uniquely—and positively—identified as a police vehicle. 4. During the 1980's, the Dodge Diplomat was *the* vehicle used by law enforcement, including this conservatively marked car from the Kansas Highway Patrol. The agency has now replaced the gold shield with a new, more modern symbol.

1

2

3

4

1

2

1. Vehicles of state law enforcement agencies are commonly identified very conservatively, which this photograph of a Maryland State Police car shows very clearly. Older models from this agency were a light tan color and had a reflective stripe along the side. A very common identifier of highway patrol vehicles used to be the number of antennas they sported, but with advanced communications technology this is no longer true. **2.** The state of Louisiana has a level of government called a Parish, which takes the place of a county, but they still have a Sheriff, and he is an important elected figure. Sheriff Steven May of Caldwell Parish in Columbia, Louisiana, has a cleanly designed patrol car.

STATE AND COUNTY POLICE CARS

1

2

1. This is a photograph of the design on the Maryland State Police patrol fleet prior to 1996. (See page 127 for the current graphic treatment.) **2.** The Cass County, Missouri, Sheriff's Department, in the heart of America, has a classically conservative but locally recognizable design. **3.** Unusual for the Midwest is this red graphic design for the St. Louis County Police Department, based in Clayton, Missouri. It is very distinctive for the area. **4.** The Minnesota State Patrol has a distinctive maroon color for its vehicles that is representative of the iron ore for which the area was so famous. This is a photograph of the design that was used for a long period before being modernized in 1992. While the graphics were changed, the unique color remains a part of the fleet's design.

3

4

STATE AND COUNTY POLICE CARS

1. In Colfax County, South Dakota, there are a lot of long, lonely stretches of highway to invite speeders. This Camaro from the Sheriff's Department was its answer to controlling traffic. 2. Police-package '91 Camaros replaced 1989 Mustangs as effective speed-control vehicles for the Nevada Highway Patrol. There weren't many vehicles on the road that could get away from the Camaros. 3. As you might expect from the New England area, this patrol vehicle for the New Hampshire State Police is the model of conservatism, from the muted dark green and copper colors of the car to the quiet, color-coordinated gold symbol on the door.

STATE AND COUNTY POLICE CARS

1

2

3

Opposite page: **1.** The extensive fleet of the Hillsborough County, Florida, Sheriff's Office includes this good-looking Dodge Intrepid. **2.** The Craven County, North Carolina, Sheriff's Office car—with its design depicting flight—is appropriately positioned. **3.** This car from the Sheriff of the County of Middlesex, New Jersey, displays bold markings. *This page:* **1.** Even the New York State Police found a need for the police-package Camaro on their highways. **2.** The Nassau County Police Department, on Long Island, New York, had these easily recognized cars on patrol. **3.** The Sheriff's Department of Laurel County, Kentucky, topped a blue Crown Vic with a matching blue lightbar.

STATE AND COUNTY POLICE CARS

This page: **1.** As mentioned previously, red on law enforcement vehicles is not common except in the Northeast, as is shown by this car for the Erie County Sheriff's Department of Buffalo, New York. **2.** The Ohio State Highway Patrol is proud of its unique symbol, which dates back to the very beginnings of the department. Silver is the department's standard color, but it has used light-colored vehicles in the past. *Opposite page:* **1.** Franklin County Sheriff Earl Smith in Columbus, Ohio, borrowed this Lamborghini from a local dealer to successfully promote his agency's anti-drug program to teenagers. **2-3.** This Oklahoma Highway Patrol Plymouth Gran Fury was used until the late 1980's. A unique feature of this agency's design is the added white patch over the rear wheel. The flag on the door is a late touch.

1

2

1

2

3

1

2

3

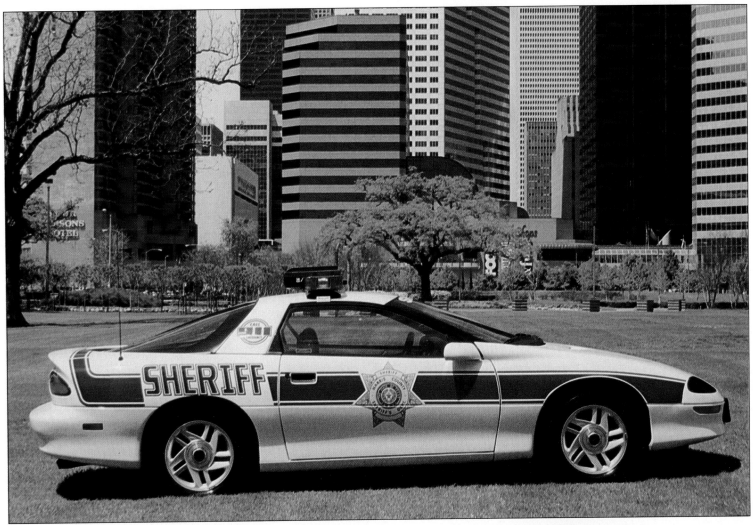

1

2

3

Opposite page: **1.** The Allegheny County, Pennsylvania, Sheriff used Chevy Luminas for patrol. **2.** The South Carolina Highway Patrol used Mustangs for traffic control. **3.** The South Dakota Highway Patrol puts pastel blue Fords on its roads. *This page:* **1.** The Harris County, Texas, Sheriff gets a lot of use from his 1996 Camaros. **2.** In El Paso County, Texas, a black-and-white Caprice patrols the roads. **3.** The Kleberg County, Texas, Sheriff originally ran Mustangs but switched to police-package Camaros.

1

1. The Fairfax County Police Department, in Fairfax, Virginia, a suburb of Washington, D.C., has a sleekly decorated blue Ford Crown Victoria on patrol duty. 2. The Sheriff of Fairfax County, whose agency is separate from the Fairfax County Police, has a distinctively different look to his patrol vehicles.

2

1

2

3

4

1. Patrol cars of the Sheriff's Office for the City of Lynchburg, Virginia, are rather commonly marked. 2. The Virginia State Police have a conservative but distinctively marked two-tone blue 1994 Caprice. They carry the blue theme even to the blue lightbar. 3. The Hanover County, Virginia, Sheriff's Office also has a blue emergency light on top, which doesn't seem to coordinate with the vehicle's brown color. 4. On the other side of the country, the vehicles of the Mason County Sheriff's Office in Shelton, Washington, are in tune with the area's lush green countryside.

1

2

1. The Kenosha County, Wisconsin, Sheriff's Department has clearly identified its patrol cars, but hiding part of the star in the wheel opening is unusual. **2.** This Caprice from the Manitowoc County, Wisconsin, Sheriff's Department is decorated in the agency's colors and graphics that were used prior to 1996. **3.** This dark Crown Victoria of the Manitowoc Sheriff sports the department's latest colors and a modern reflective design.

3

1

1. The Sheriff of Cabell County, West Virginia, has used modern reflective materials to good advantage on his vehicle fleet.
2. The West Virginia State Police changed their vehicle graphics in 1995 to reflect a more modern agency, testing them on both dark- and light-colored cars. The dark blue Caprice wears a gold top, while the white Crown Victoria has the police identification in reverse at the top of its windshield.

2

CHAPTER FIVE
SPECIAL USE VEHICLES

The jurisdiction of the law enforcement agency, be it municipal, county, or state, will determine the variety of vehicles and the number of units in its fleet. The largest departments might have a dozen or more special use vehicles available.

While state agencies patrolling the wide-open spaces of the West have employed pursuit-type cars for many years, only in the past decade have such vehicles been accepted by urban agencies. The California Highway Patrol (CHP) was responsible for Ford developing the 1982 Mustang Police Special and promoting its ability to catch any speeder on the highway. It was the first effective pursuit vehicle with a police package that was affordable by all.

Chevrolet entered the competition with its Camaro and successfully gained a share of the business, but various departments considered other makes, such as the Pontiac Firebird and the Dodge Daytona. All these cars were fast but severely limited in interior space, which caused problems in transporting prisoners and in finding room for radios, radars, computers, and video cameras.

Use of these small pursuit vehicles declined when Chevrolet introduced its newly designed 1991 full-size Caprice with a police package. Its performance compared favorably with the smaller cars—in handling as well as speed—and officers preferred its spaciousness. But with the demise of the Caprice in 1996, the smaller cars will likely gain in popularity again, as the police-package Ford Crown Victoria doesn't offer the same level of performance.

Law enforcement agencies have tried various four-wheel-drive vehicles, and many are impressed with their performance. The primary contender in this category has been the Jeep Cherokee, which is offered with a police package. A four-door Geo Tracker was also available with a police package in 1996 but generated little interest. However, Chevrolet has announced that it will offer its Tahoe with a police package in 1997, hoping it will rival the departed Caprice in popularity.

A special use vehicle that has seen somewhat of a rebirth of late is the motorcycle. While some departments have always had some cycles around for various duties such as parades, more are now assigning them regularly to patrol. Even state agencies other than the famous CHP have added them to their fleets after many years. The Illinois State Police and the Michigan State Police both use Harley-Davidsons to patrol the interstate highways running through metropolitan areas such as Chicago and Detroit. A motorcycle offshoot seeing service with many police agencies that have parks or waterfronts within their jurisdictions is the four-wheel ATV.

Agencies with waterways commonly include boats in their transportation fleets to enforce safety on the water. These craft are mostly standard pleasure boats, averaging in size from 20 to 24 feet, which have been outfitted with police identification. In addition, some agencies have added personal watercraft (a.k.a. Jet Skis) to their fleets.

Almost any vehicle you can name has been used by some police agency in some manner. Bicycle patrols are popular now, and some agencies have even pressed golf carts into service. If it has wheels or an engine, some agency has very likely put a police badge on it.

SPECIAL USE VEHICLES

1

2

3

Previous page: A Ford Explorer police unit is shown outside the Public Safety Building in Rogers, Arkansas. *This page:* **1.** The Oceanside, California, Police Department Beach Team makes good use of the capabilities of both the Jeep and the ATV to navigate its sandy beaches. **2.** To patrol its stretches of beaches and paved paths, the Monterey Police Department in California uses a Suzuki Sidekick and a Raleigh bicycle. **3.** This Corvette Stingray from the Livermore, California, Police doesn't get out on street patrol very much, but it does get the attention of young people whom the department wants to reach with a message. **4.** The Chula Vista, California, Police Department's hot rod is maintained by the agency's reserve officers and appears at many public events as an attention-getter.

4

1

2

1. This Saleen Mustang from the Seal Beach, California, Police Department makes for an intimidating patrol car. Regularly assigned to traffic control duties, it has a special transmission, a lower rear-end ratio, and 16-inch tires on alloy rims. Saleen, which called this car their SB/S (for Seal Beach Special), developed it as a possible offering to the law enforcement market. **2.** The SB/S has outstanding acceleration, handy for catching speeders in a metropolitan area. **3.** The St. Pete Beach, Florida, Police Department uses a front-wheel-drive Ford Taurus and a four-wheel-drive Ford Explorer to patrol its oceanfront jurisdiction. The jumping dolphin is a nice touch in the agency's graphics.

3

SPECIAL USE VEHICLES

1

2

3

1. These officers driving the Kawasaki ATVs for the Ft. Meade, Florida, Police Department look like they have a pleasurable assignment. **2.** If you're going to spend much time patrolling on an ATV, you had better be dressed for the occasion. The special T-shirts are appropriate for the job. **3.** Traffic enforcement for the Jupiter, Florida, Police Department seems to be well patrolled with this shiny and fully identified Chevrolet Camaro. The graphic figure beside the door window has a double message: "Safe & Sober" is a reminder to use seat belts and not to drive under the influence. **4.** Jupiter's traffic enforcement is supported with this gleaming Harley-Davidson police motorcycle.

4

1

2

3

4

1. In order to provide adequate community services, the Sarasota County, Florida, Sheriff's Office provides its civilian aides with an appropriately marked S-10 Blazer for their transportation needs. The lightbar is correctly equipped with only yellow caution lights. **2.** A full-size Ford Bronco, equipped with an expensive chromed push bar in front, gets the Margate, Florida, police into areas that might be difficult for regular patrol cruisers to reach. **3.** This two-door Geo Tracker from the City of Hollywood, Florida, Police predates the police-package four-door Tracker introduced by Chevrolet in 1996, but it is the type of vehicle needed for the local sandy beach terrain. **4.** While the metropolitan area of Miami is mostly paved, some areas patrolled by the Metro-Dade Police Department are beaches and other difficult-to-reach areas that are only accessible to special vehicles such as this Yamaha ATV.

SPECIAL USE VEHICLES

1

2

1. While this Caprice is boldly identified as a police vehicle, it serves as transportation for the Lake Park, Florida, Police Department's Community Response Team, which, as noted in smaller type on the front fender, is "In partnership with our community." The dark film on the windows and the special wheels certainly set the car apart from most patrol vehicles. **2.** Just a quick look should tell people that this Camaro was seized from a drug dealer and is now a police vehicle for the Lady Lake, Florida, Police Department. **3.** The offset blue and red stripes are nicely adapted to the contours of the Lady Lake police car. The heavily tinted windows would not be legal in some parts of the country.

3

1

2

3

4

1. This bright Corvette, also confiscated from a drug dealer, is not assigned to regular patrol duties by the Waterloo, Iowa, Police Department, but it does get a lot of attention when it hits the streets on the way to public events. **2.** This black GMC Jimmy carries the colors of the Burns Harbor, Indiana, Police Department. **3.** The Peachtree City, Georgia, Police Department uses this prominently marked Ford Mustang for patrol duties. **4.** The markings on this Crown Vic from the Jackson County, Indiana, Sheriff's Department are certainly innovative and attract attention to its special message of using seat belts.

SPECIAL USE VEHICLES

1

2

1. While it isn't possible to ride motorcycles throughout the year in Illinois due to the snow and freezing conditions, the Homewood Police Department, in a suburb of Chicago, makes good use of their fully outfitted Harley-Davidson for traffic enforcement duties. **2.** Even from the rear, the Homewood motorcycle is obviously a police vehicle. The many emergency lights are especially important for the safety of the motor officer during a traffic stop. **3.** The Lincolnwood Police Department, in another suburb of Chicago, also puts a Harley-Davidson motorcycle on traffic duty. **4.** The Sedgwick County Sheriff's Department, in Wichita, Kansas, has applied the same distinctive design very effectively to all its vehicles, from patrol cars to support vehicles such as this Chevy Astro van that is used by a service officer. **5.** While the soft-top two-door Geo Tracker is very popular in agencies with waterfronts to patrol, in the colder climes of Wichita, Kansas, the Police Department finds this hard-top Tracker a better choice as a service vehicle.

3

4

5

1

2

3

1-3. Posed along the recently restored waterfront of Baltimore, Maryland, this sleek-looking Corvette from the Baltimore Police Department is suitably marked as having been forfeited by a drug dealer. The lightbar on top of this 1988 Corvette is a short unit specially developed for the small pursuit vehicles so popular of late with many departments.

SPECIAL USE VEHICLES

1

2

3

1. A red Thunderbird would be unusual in any police department, but the fact that Taylor, Michigan, is neighbor to Dearborn (home of the Ford Motor Company) might account for the local police using such a vehicle to patrol its streets. 2. The Ferndale, Michigan, Police Department has made its Ford Explorer a very patriotic vehicle for traffic control efforts. 3. The Gulfport, Mississippi, Police Department has a well-equipped and very attractively painted Harley-Davidson motorcycle. Note the radar head mounted prominently on the windshield. 4. Out in the prairie lands of Nebraska, the Platte County Sheriff's Department probably gets a lot of good use from its Mustang pursuit car. 5. The Department of Police for the city of Perth Amboy, New Jersey, was not overly creative in developing the graphic scheme for its Dodge extended van, but there's no doubt about it being a police vehicle.

4

5

1

2

1. The New York State Police have got it all: Caprices, Camaros, Mustangs—even a helicopter. As is traditional with state police agencies, this department has conservative graphics for its vehicles. An interesting point is how they are equipped: the Camaro has one spotlight, the Caprice has two spotlights, and the Mustang has none. Perhaps the take-down lights in the lightbars are sufficient illumination for the pursuit cars. **2.** In way-up-north New York state, it is not that unusual for half of a fleet of vehicles to be snowmobiles, as is shown here for the Town of Webb Police Department.

SPECIAL USE VEHICLES

1. This three-wheeled Cushman vehicle does odd jobs, like checking the parking meters, for the Tonawanda, New York, Police. **2.** The Parma, Ohio, Police like their bright red IROC-Z Camaro. **3.** The Medford, Oregon, Police use their Corvette in crime prevention programs.

1

3

2

1. Blue and gold are popular colors for police graphics. The Upper Providence Township Police, of Media, Pennsylvania, also use this Z28 Camaro for their D.A.R.E. program. **2.** The Upper Gwynedd Township Police, of West Point, Pennsylvania, applied unique striping to their Caprice. **3.** The Hartsville Public Safety Department, in South Carolina, has a well-marked Crown Vic for its Community Officer.

1

1. While it is certainly not a police-package pursuit vehicle, this classic 1967 Camaro, acquired through a drug forfeiture by the Richardson, Texas, Police Department, captures the attention of youths in that area. Note the tastefully applied blue graphics and matching lightbar. **2.** This four-door Suzuki Sidekick is all the car the Corpus Christi State University Police Department needs to patrol the campus.

2

1

2

1. It's not your usual black-and-white police car, but this Corvette is likely to be just as effective as any police-package Caprice in deterring speeders for the Coppell, Texas, Police Department. **2.** Another good-looking Harley-Davidson motorcycle, this time in brown, comes from the Prince William County, Virginia, Sheriff's Office in Manassas.

SPECIAL USE VEHICLES

1

2

1. The Wythe County, Virginia, Sheriff's Office did a fine job of coordinating state-mandated colors and design with the body shape of this 1993 Mustang, especially in flowing the light color over the spoiler on the trunk lid. In addition to the standard police equipment, these Mustangs have HAWK radars, an in-car video system, and a radar-detector detector. **2.** NASA Security doesn't need a full-size patrol vehicle to keep tabs on its Washington, D.C., headquarters, so this small four-wheeled vehicle is adequate for the job. The lightbar on top is a nice touch. **3.** You wouldn't think that Moses Lake, Washington (population 11,000), would need a full-size Caprice to manage traffic, but the Police Department has a well-identified car assigned for that purpose.

3

1

2

1. The U.S. Border Patrol is about the only law enforcement agency that can afford a Hummer, which has proven to be an effective police vehicle in tough terrain. **2.** The Border Patrol also uses full-size Ford Broncos in many areas that require off-road patrolling.

SPECIAL USE VEHICLES

1

This page: **1.** It is obvious that the Canadian Pacific Railway Company has the service of a creative art director who has the freedom to be innovative. The graphics on this Lumina from the railroad's police department are conservative yet imaginative and fit the application perfectly. **2.** The Sault Ste. Marie Police Service in Ontario, Canada, has assigned a Nissan Axxess minivan to its local R.I.D.E. program (Reduce Impaired Driving Everywhere). The vehicle was donated by a local dealer. *Opposite page:* **1-2.** This Range Rover from the Greater Manchester Police in England is marked with their old design. The new graphics, which feature large blocks of bold reflective colors, are the result of an effort to develop a national livery which will be adopted in some manner by each local police force. **3.** The rear of the Range Rover has a large reflective message panel.

2

1

2

3

SPECIAL USE VEHICLES

1

2

3

This page: **1.** This Land Rover Discovery serves the Greater Manchester, England, Police. **2-3.** A Mercedes G300 was tested by the Surrey, England, Police. *Opposite page:* **1.** This Land Rover Defender is from the Strathclyde, Scotland, Police.

1

SPECIAL USE VEHICLES

1

2

3

1. This Lotus Esprit Turbo carries the proposed new national livery for English police vehicles. The "Concept" car is equipped with in-car video, VASCAR, and TRACKER. **2.** Police-special BMW motorcycles are popular with law enforcement agencies in England. This one is clearly marked for the Devon & Cornwall Constabulary. **3.** The Northumbria Police in England patrol in spirited Ford Escort RS Cosworths.

1

2

3

1-3. The bold, distinctive design on these vehicles for the Dutch National Police was selected because it met the established criteria of optimum visibility both during daylight and at night. It is also favored for its flexibility (the same striping is applied to 170 different police vehicles, from motorcycles and trucks to boats), and for its ease of application. It is also a unique design that is easily recognized by international visitors. The Politie has a fleet of Porsches and BMW motorcycles assigned to patrol duties.

CHAPTER SIX
SUPPORT VEHICLES

As in many business operations, a number of different vehicles may be needed to fulfill the variety of duties assigned to a law enforcement agency. The functions requiring special vehicles were covered in the preceding chapter, but there are many more mundane chores that can be readily handled by standard production vehicles.

A good example of this can be found in departments that have canine units. While some simply remove the back seat of a standard sedan or station wagon to make room for the dogs, others perform some slight modifications, such as installing a special cage or platform. Some even add a special remote-controlled door opener. Because of liability concerns, most agencies clearly identify their K-9 mobile units with warning messages. For a touch of individuality, some officers paint their dog's likeness and name on the vehicle.

BATmobiles—not for Batman and Robin, but rather for administering DUI tests—are used by some agencies. Many departments with programs attacking drunk driving have outfitted a vehicle with the necessary testing equipment, allowing tests to be performed at various locations. Some of the vehicles have facilities for testing both breath and blood, as well as for confining those who fail the tests. Having equipment on the scene frees up officers from having to transport offenders long distances for tests.

Among the more exotic vehicles some departments have available are armored cars, but they are too expensive and underutilized for most agencies to include in their fleets. Many are converted money-transfer trucks from firms such as Brinks, while others are ex-military armored vehicles obtained from the armed forces. Few ever see action except as part of a SWAT training exercise or as a parade vehicle.

A vehicle that gets little notice—but performs a very important function—is the Command Center. Some are little more than a converted van with a mobile telephone, while others are much more elaborate, with a wide array of communications facilities, conference areas, and washrooms. They come in all sizes and shapes, but their purpose is the same: to provide a central location for supervising an operation, be it SWAT, a natural disaster, or a community relations event.

Vehicles used in the collection of evidence at crime scenes may contain everything from basic fingerprinting items to extensive photography and video equipment. Some of these vehicles are also outfitted for use in accident reconstruction.

Large agencies such as the New York City Police Department have entire divisions assigned to emergency response activities. These units consist of special teams of officers able to handle any event, along with suitably equipped trucks. Most smaller agencies are only able to outfit certain special units for specific activities such as bomb disposal or water rescue.

Some support vehicles are common to most agencies, such as "paddy wagons," now formally identified as Prisoner Transportation Vehicles. In Chicago, these specially made trucks are called "Squadrols," and they perform a variety of tasks.

Another important vehicle to many police agencies, particularly in larger cities, is the tow truck. These are used not only to assist the department's fleet, but also to remove illegally parked vehicles or those impounded as part of a criminal case.

In short, support vehicles can take on many different forms; the scope is limited only by the duties of a particular agency.

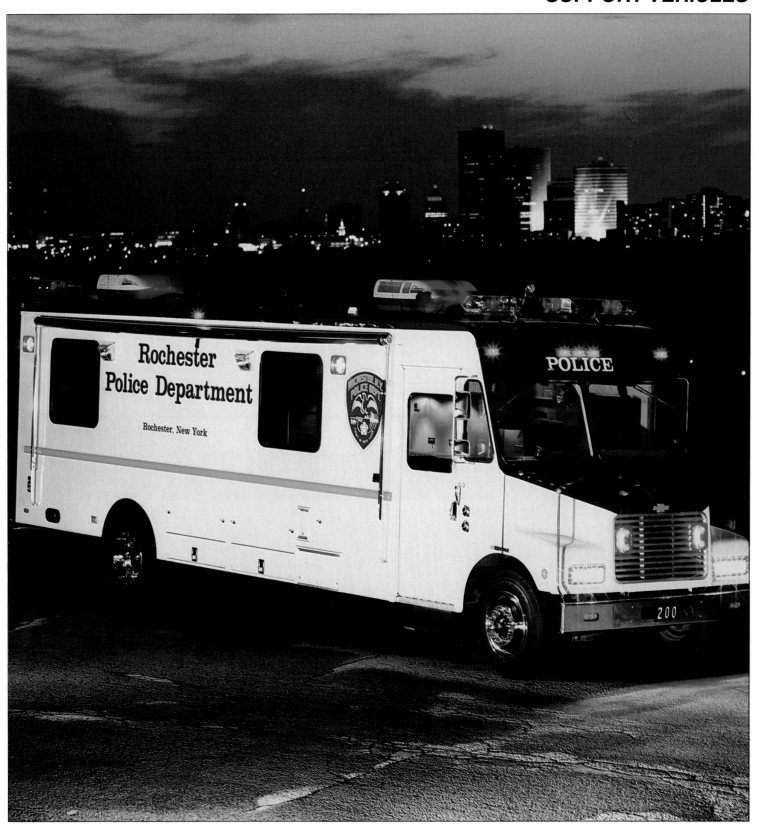

SUPPORT VEHICLES

1

2

Previous page: Rochester, New York, Police make use of this well-equipped mobile command center. This page: **1.** Sheriffs' departments probably have more use for trucks than municipal agencies, but this Ford F350 four-wheel-drive CrewCab pickup from the Tuscaloosa County, Alabama, Sheriff's Office reflects the public's current interest in trucks. Note the chrome grille guard and winch. **2.** The Scottsdale, Arizona, Police Department answers emergency calls with this Chevy utility truck. **3-4.** This mobile command center for the Pima County, Arizona, Sheriff's Department is fully equipped to respond quickly to any disaster call within the jurisdiction. Due to the extremely hot temperatures encountered in that area, the unit requires three high-capacity, roof-mounted air conditioners.

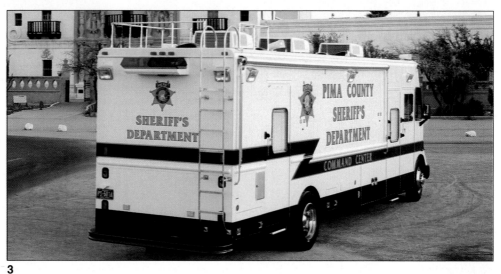

3

4

1

2

1-2. This modified Chevrolet pickup truck from the West Covina, California, Police Department has been painted to match other vehicles in the agency's fleet. It is equipped to handle traffic problems that might be encountered at a major collision scene, carrying lights, flares, and traffic cones. **3.** The Irvine, California, Police Department provides its canine unit with a Ford Explorer.

3

1

2

3

1. The Los Angeles County, California, Sheriff's Department covers a wide area, and its Field Sergeants must be equipped to handle a variety of tasks. This Chevy Suburban is heavily loaded with gear, including a canopy and chairs, an electricity generator, scuba equipment, and a well-stocked first aid kit. **2.** The Suburban's front console has all the latest communications equipment. **3.** Everything a Command Sergeant needs is in the neatly organized rear console, including extra communications units.

1

2

3

1. Special response teams need special equipment that does not fit easily into regular patrol vehicles. Therefore, agencies have developed various truck configurations for this task, such as this Ford from the New Castle County, Delaware, Division of Police. **2.** This Pontiac mini-van is routinely assigned to community service calls, but it is equipped for patrol duty if required by the Azusa, California, Police Department. **3.** The Metro Dade Police Department, in Miami, Florida, puts this converted city bus to good use as a mobile command post.

SUPPORT VEHICLES

1

2

3

1. King, the Panama City, Florida, canine, is transported in a very nice Jeep. He even has his photograph on the rear side windows. **2.** The canine for the North Miami Beach Police Department enjoys similar accommodations. **3.** The communications/control tree in the North Miami Beach Jeep is easily accessible, but it lacks the portable computer that would normally be mounted on the top plate.

1. The Marion County Sheriff's Department, in Ocala, Florida, has done a good job of putting together a new graphics program for its vehicle fleet. It has developed a design that can be applied equally well to a diverse collection of vehicles, including this Peacekeeper armored car. **2.** The versatility of the design is evident in its application to this bomb containment trailer. **3.** Even on large vehicles, such as this SWAT van, the design is consistent and just as impressive in providing the right image for the department.

1

2

1. Not every police agency has the funds to purchase a special vehicle for their canine unit. The East Hampton, Connecticut, Police Department converted one of its regular Ford Crown Vic patrol cars for this duty.
2. The newly created Jamaica Police Force needs the tough capability of the Toyota Land Cruiser II to navigate some of its poorly maintained roads. 3. The Town of Normal, Illinois, is not a big place, but it has a lot of students from Illinois State University who keep this Breath Alcohol Testing Mobile Unit busy.

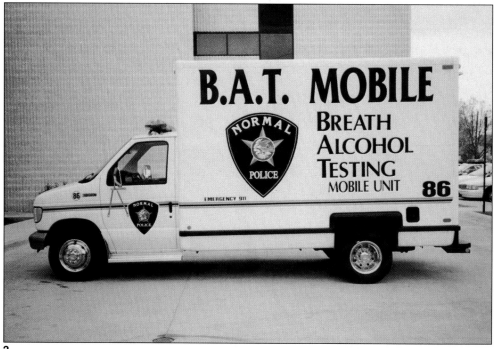

3

SUPPORT VEHICLES

1. The Salem Police Department, in Marion County, Illinois, uses a Ford Bronco for its canine unit. **2.** This Chevy Suburban from the East Moline, Illinois, Police Department is the agency's emergency response vehicle and is outfitted to provide all the equipment necessary for most emergency service calls. **3.** When this shining hulk of a vehicle for the Northern Illinois Police Alarm System Emergency Service Team blasts down a road with lights and sirens activated, the road clears. It serves as the SWAT command post for 23 Chicago suburbs.

1

2

3

SUPPORT VEHICLES

1. This Mobile Command Vehicle for the Illinois State Police was delivered in 1994, and has since been called into service around the state at disaster scenes and public events such as the World Cup Soccer Games and the Democratic National Convention. The agency faced a dilemma in decorating the unit: how to stripe a vehicle two patrol cars long and two patrol cars high while keeping it identifiable. **2.** The State Police had the rear of this vehicle painted red to make it more easily seen while parked alongside the roadway for a vehicle safety inspection stop. A special staff is assigned to this unit because of its complexity due to the many different functions it is assigned. It has nine land-based telephone lines, various radios, several computers, a 20-kilowatt gas-powered generator, an extendable mast for a 360-degree-view video camera, and even a small weather station.

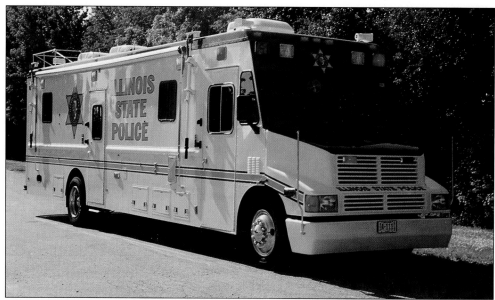

1

2

1

2

4

5

3

1. For emergency service calls in the Huntington County, Indiana, area, this International rescue truck from the Sheriff's Department is sure to be on the scene quickly. **2.** The Huntington, Indiana, rescue truck, in the state-mandated colors, provides the necessary tools to effect a rescue, though it is not an ambulance. **3.** This Ford Econoline van conversion from the Sedgwick County, Kansas, Sheriff's Department needs a special generator to power all the lights—especially that super lightbar in front. **4.** The Lake County, Indiana, Sheriff's Department needs a Mobile Crime Lab to handle all the service calls generated in the populous Chicago-Gary area. **5.** This Dragon Wagon, an extended Ford van, serves the Waterloo, Iowa, Police for prisoner transport.

SUPPORT VEHICLES

1. The Louisville, Kentucky, SWAT equipment truck is a specially modified Ford Econoline with dual rear wheels. **2.** "A place for everything, and everything in its place" must be the motto for the Louisville SWAT team. These side compartments are designed to be securely locked. **3.** The team's weapons and munitions are securely stored yet readily available when needed. **4.** Easy access is a key requirement for a SWAT team going into action, and this vehicle answers that need. **5.** The interior of the vehicle is designed for efficiency. Passenger comfort is secondary, but adequate.

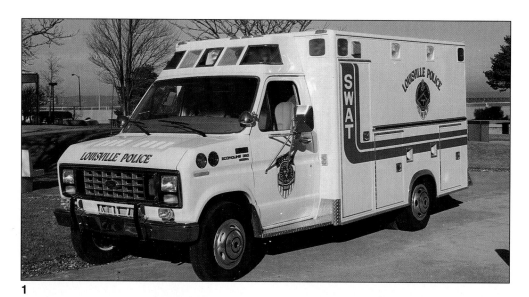

1

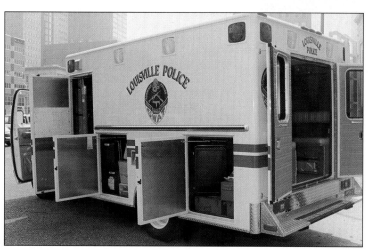

2

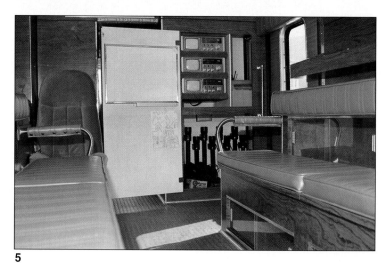

3

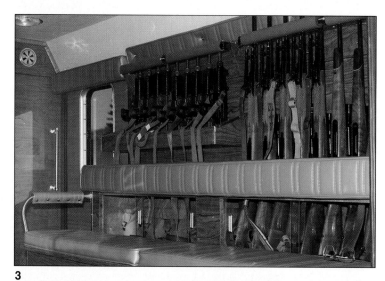

4

5

1

2

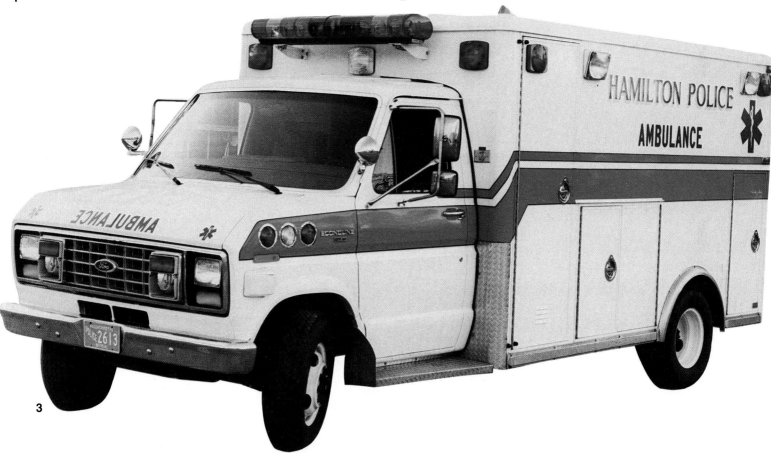

3

1. The police department in Kenner, Louisiana, just outside of New Orleans, has a traditionally marked Oldsmobile Station Wagon for their crime scene support vehicle. **2.** The Causeway Police Department of the Greater New Orleans Expressway Commission patrols the long bridge across Lake Pontchartrain, which provides ample opportunity to use this tow truck. An illustration of the jurisdiction is painted on its sides. **3.** The Hamilton, Massachusetts, Police Department ambulance has an ample supply of lights to illuminate the night.

1

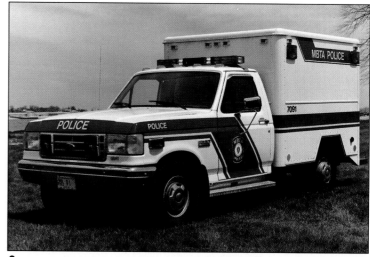

2

3

4

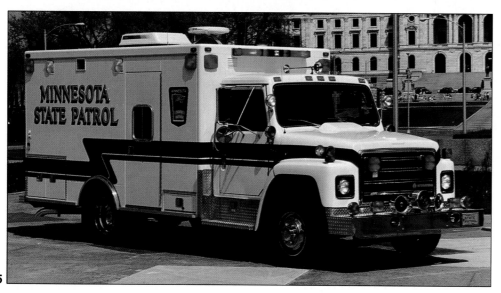

5

1-2. The Massachusetts Bay Transit Authority, located in Boston, has a cleanly marked and well-lighted Ford truck that serves many needs, including the transport of prisoners. **3.** The Baltimore, Maryland, Police obtained a military-surplus 2½-ton truck and cleaned it up nicely for their calls requiring heavy-duty response. **4.** In a suburb of Minneapolis, the police department for the city of Maple Grove, Minnesota, probably doesn't have a lot of calls that require putting this Peacekeeper armored car into action, but as the saying goes, it's better to be safe than sorry. **5.** The Minnesota State Patrol uses this International truck as a special-purpose vehicle to provide support for a variety of emergencies.

SUPPORT VEHICLES

1. The Sheriff's Department for Lewis and Clark County, Montana, very likely puts a lot of miles on this Chevrolet Astro van, which has been converted into a prisoner transport vehicle. **2.** In Missouri, the St. Louis Metropolitan Police Department modified a standard ambulance van into a special Breath Alcohol Testing mobile unit. **3.** The New Hampshire State Police customized this HRC Imperial mobile home into a spacious and well-appointed command and communications center.

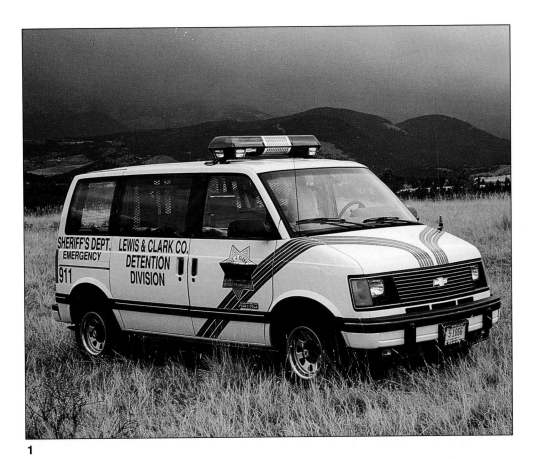

1

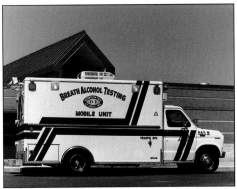

2

3

SUPPORT VEHICLES

1

2

1. The Pleasantville, New Jersey, Police Department made this Jeep into their canine vehicle and made sure that the public was well aware of its assignment. **2.** The South Plainfield, New Jersey, Police Department uses this restored International Harvester van to transport its Honor Guard. **3.** The Police Athletic League sponsored by the Nashua, New Hampshire, Police Department, is very active and requires a sizable truck to move its equipment around. **4.** Sobriety Checkpoints require a lot of extra safety equipment, so the Taos, New Mexico, Police Department acquired a Chevy S-10 pickup and trailer to transport the items between locations. The graphic design reflects the Native American influence prominent in the area.

3

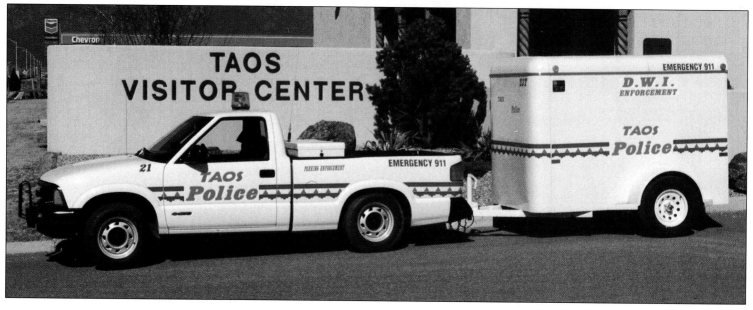

4

1. This extended-body Chevrolet Sportvan from the Farmington, New Mexico, Police Department is well identified for its assigned duties. **2-3.** An ex-military V-100 armored vehicle serves the New York Port Authority. **4.** The New York City Transit Police Department, which was merged into the New York City Police Department in 1995, had a customized city bus as an effective Mobile Arrest Processing Center.

SUPPORT VEHICLES

1

2

1. The Erie County Sheriff's Department, in Buffalo, New York, is ready for heavy action with this surplus six-wheel-drive military armored car. It is one of three such vehicles available. **2.** The New York City Police Department developed a graphic design that is effective on all its many vehicles, including this motorcycle maintenance truck. **3.** As part of its special equipment, the New Rochelle Police Department Mobile Precinct vehicle has a telescoping light that can be raised to provide extra illumination over a wide area. **4.** Many metropolitan police forces, like the one in Columbus, Ohio, have found advantages to having their own tow trucks.

3

4

1. This Columbus, Ohio, Police Department International truck is equipped for heavy-duty towing of both parking violators and cars damaged in collisions. **2.** This large GMC service van is another good example of how the New York City Police Department's graphic design is applied effectively to many different vehicles. **3.** Not all confiscated vehicles become customized D.A.R.E. cars. The Henderson County, North Carolina, Sheriff's Department assigned this 1985 Chevrolet Station Wagon to their Victim Services section, and decorated it appropriately. Note the illustration of a helping hand on the hood. **4.** Not all special response police units are called SWAT. The Chambersburg, Pennsylvania, Police Department has a Special Emergency Team instead, which is served by this large Chevrolet van.

1

2

3

4

SUPPORT VEHICLES

1-2. When the South Carolina State Police set up a sobriety checkpoint or support a local police department with a DUI problem, this Chevrolet medium-duty truck answers the call. The vehicle doesn't have very exciting graphics, which is typical of many state agencies, but there is little doubt as to its intended mission. The multitude of external lights provides ample nighttime illumination.

1

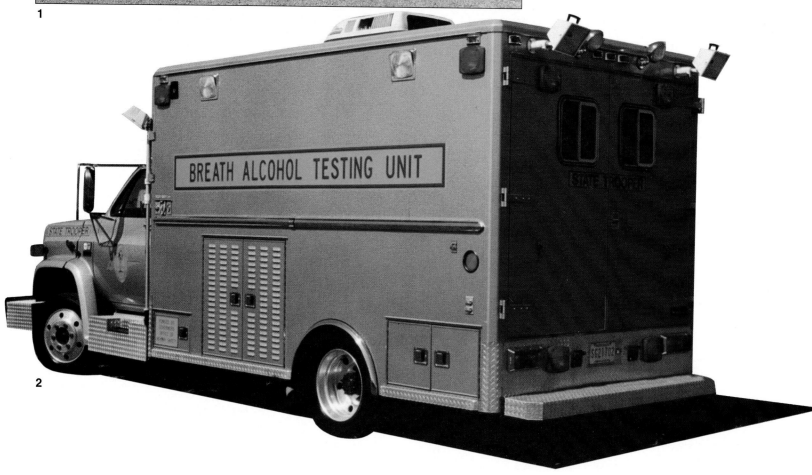

2

1

2

3

1. The Kleberg County, Texas, Sheriff's Department evidently has a good-looking vehicle for every purpose. **2.** The Charleston, South Carolina, Police regularly get calls for underwater recovery, and they need a large van to transport the necessary equipment. **3.** The Metropolitan Police Department in Washington, D.C., converted a city bus into a mobile command center.

SUPPORT VEHICLES

1. There's a lot of water to patrol in its jurisdiction, and the Tennessee Valley Authority needs to access it quickly at different points. As a result, this Suburban with a boat and trailer is a very practical unit for them.
2. The Metropolitan Police Department, one of four law enforcement agencies with jurisdiction in Washington, D.C., has a capable and experienced mobile bomb disposal team always on the ready. **3.** Controlling parking on federal grounds is a continuing problem that the U.S. Capitol Police handle with the aid of this Chevy tow truck.

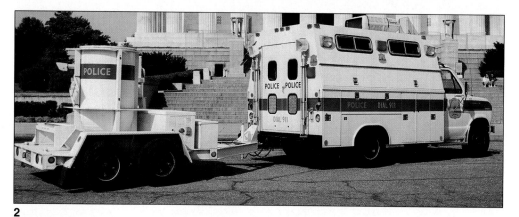

1

2

1.The U.S. Capitol Police have jurisdiction over all federal grounds and property in Washington, D.C. This Chevrolet bomb truck, just one of the special vehicles in the fleet, transports a bomb robot behind the cab. 2. This U.S. Capitol Police explosives truck is not one that you want to follow. 3. The U.S. Capitol Police have a variety of dogs trained for different special activities—drugs, explosives, etc.—and they need a large truck to accommodate them on assignment.

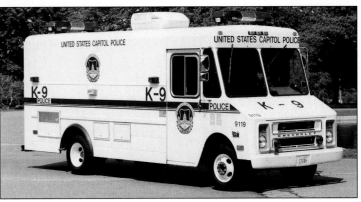

3

1

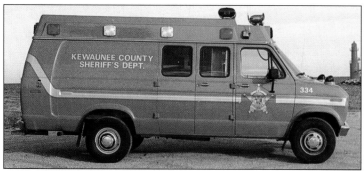

2

This page: **1.** What might be a bomb truck to some police agencies is a Hazardous Devices Unit to others, as shown by this GMC van from the King County, Washington, Police Department. **2-3.** The Kewaunee County, Wisconsin, Sheriff's Department has two emergency response vehicles, both of which appear to be customized ambulance-type vehicles. *Opposite page:* **1-2.** This RAP vehicle (Racine Alcohol Patrol) from the Racine, Wisconsin, Police Department was professionally designed, both inside and out, and entered service with the department in 1990.

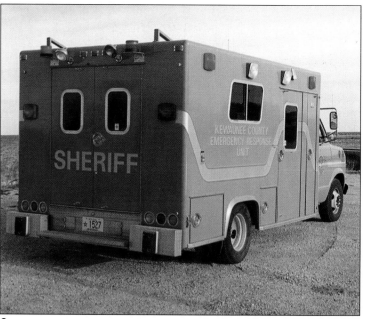

3

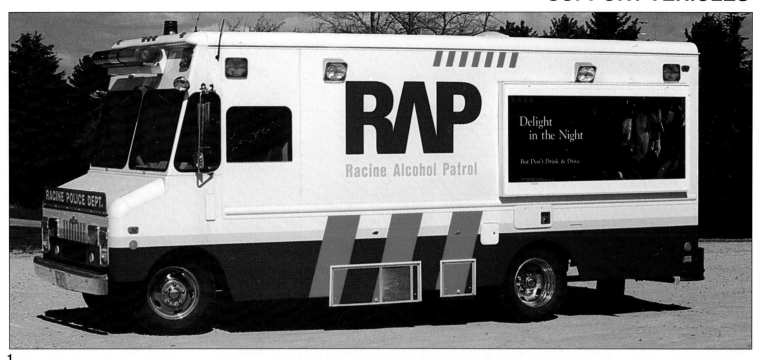

1

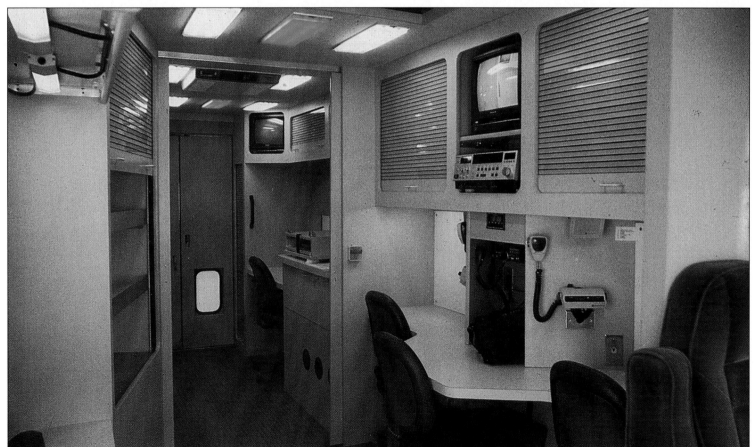

2

SUPPORT VEHICLES

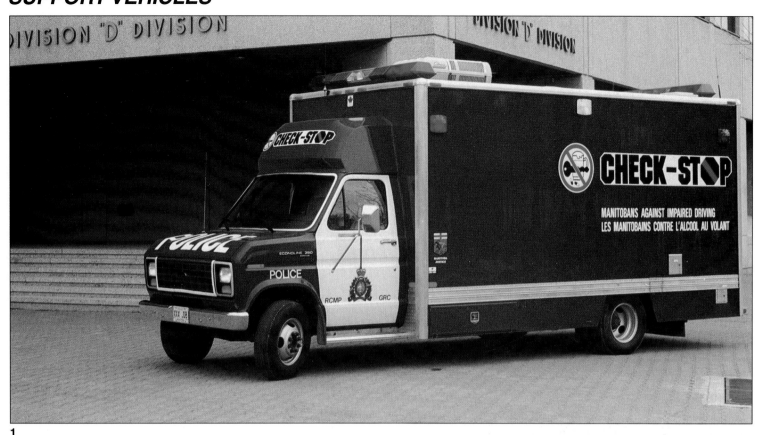

1

1-2. This CHECK-STOP Ford Econoline van from the Royal Canadian Mounted Police post in Winnipeg, Manitoba, is not as finely designed as Racine's RAP unit on the previous page, but it accomplishes the same objective—getting impaired drivers off the road. As is common in Canada, wording is also written in French.

2

SUPPORT VEHICLES

1

1. This Z-Class Prisoner Transport truck from Sheriff Services in the Province of British Columbia, Canada, is a Chevy van that was specially customized to carry prisoners and is well marked for safety. **2.** The Fredericton Police Force, in New Brunswick, Canada, converted this mobile home into a mobile center for community-oriented policing. The illustration on the side leaves no doubt as to the purpose of the vehicle. **3.** This Ford Transit Van, from the Kent County Constabulary in England, is used to transport officers to action scenes. In riot conditions, screens are inserted over the glass areas. **4.** This vehicle for the Policia Nacional, Madrid, Spain, is for transporting people—either officers or prisoners.

2

3

4

CHAPTER SEVEN

GRAPHICS FOR THE FUTURE

While those of a creative nature are likely to see the future in a rather uninhibited or even fanciful manner, law enforcement personnel tend to be a bit more conservative, most being hidebound traditionalists who look upon change with a certain degree of suspicion. But that's not to say that changes aren't taking place in law enforcement. In some areas, dramatic change has already occurred and there is optimism for further important developments, such as in the graphic design of police vehicles.

The current decade has seen police vehicles for many departments bloom as colorfully as a flower in springtime. Even agencies restricted by mandates governing what colors and graphics they must apply to their vehicles are introducing innovative new designs. The old television favorite (resulting from the California standard) of a black car with white doors and a star decal is rapidly losing favor, the common replacement being a white car with multi-colored modern graphics.

While a change in police philosophy accounts for some of these changes, another development has been just as influential: The cost of applying graphics to an automobile has become eminently more affordable. Even complicated designs can be developed quickly and inexpensively via computer and then transferred to decal film that can be easily applied to a vehicle. This means that creativity can soar, being limited only by one's imagination—and the agency's budget.

Certain design trends are beginning to develop, including more dramatic appearances, nontraditional bright colors, and unusual design effects such as three-dimensional or photographic images. There will also be improved integration of elements such as striping and lettering, along with the greater use of emblems and insignias as secondary elements rather than primary ones.

There will also be innovations in the use of reflective materials that will increase the safety of officers. While there are currently some limitations as to the colors available in reflective materials, the choices will surely broaden to a wide range of hues that will open new vistas of design.

Another element that will influence the future of police graphics is the physical shape of the vehicles. In the early '90s, the old boxy-looking Chevrolet Caprice and Ford Crown Victoria were replaced by restyled versions featuring more modern, rounded profiles. While these were not immediately popular, they eventually prompted a significant change in graphic designs; the straight lines agencies were so familiar with were now all rolling and curvy.

While this trend will likely continue as auto manufacturers progress toward the perfect aerodynamic egg shape for their passenger cars, another question looms: What about the new sport-utility vehicles (SUVs) that are becoming more and more common? Auto manufacturers are increasingly offering these truck-like vehicles with police packages, and they are sure to become more popular as officers become acquainted with their greater roominess and increased visibility. Departments will be faced with the challenge of developing graphics that fit both egg-shaped cars and boxy SUVs—or choosing separate designs.

Whatever the answer, the future is sure to be one of brighter colors and bolder, more innovative graphics. As these are phased in, the traditional "black-and-white" may appear only in old movies and television reruns.

GRAPHICS FOR THE FUTURE

Courtesy of Grafix Shoppe

Courtesy of Grafix Shoppe

Courtesy of Grafix Shoppe

Previous page: Intended to appeal to grade-school children, Darren the Lion is a new national mascot for the Drug Awareness and Resistance Education (D.A.R.E.) program. He's pictured on a Chevrolet Astro minivan drawn by Grafix Shoppe, in Eagan, Minnesota. *This page:* **1-3.** This trio of Crown Vic illustrations displays contemporary graphic designs.

1

2

Courtesy of Grafix Shoppe

3

Courtesy of Grafix Shoppe

4

Courtesy of Grafix Shoppe

1. Another Grafix Shoppe illustration dresses a Camaro with splashy D.A.R.E. graphics. Modern graphic treatments can really spruce up a plain white vehicle, as shown by (**2**) a Chevrolet Blazer, (**3**) a Ford Crown Vic, (**4**) a Chevrolet Cavalier, and (**5**) a Ford Explorer.

5

Courtesy of Grafix Shoppe

GRAPHICS FOR THE FUTURE

1. Graphics that fade from one color into another will likely become commonplace in future designs. **2.** Shades of silver and black set off the blue accents on this modern-looking black-and-white. **3.** An older Crown Vic is the basis for this patriotic D.A.R.E. design. **4.** Obviously drawn before the announced demise of the Chevrolet Caprice, this stripe-intensive rendering adds a colorful touch to the popular sedan.

GS-9216
GS-9216R

RECOMMENDED COLORS

GS-9216 (Non-reflective)
Intense Blue
& Olympic Blue

GS-9216R (Reflective)
Light Blue Scotchlite
& Gold Metallic

1 Courtesy of Grafix Shoppe

RECOMMENDED COLORS

GS-9217
(Non-reflective)
Light Navy
& Slate Metallic

GS-9217R
(Reflective)
Dark Blue Scotchlite
& Slate Metallic

GS-9218
GS-9218R

RECOMMENDED COLORS

GS-9218 (Non-reflective)
Dark Blue Metallic
& Bright Blue Metallic

GS-9218R (Reflective)
Dark Blue Scotchlite
& Bright Blue Met.

PRICING INFORMATION

Kit No.	Recommended Color(s)	Price per car	Kit No.	Recommended Color(s)	Price per car
GS-9212	Light Navy & Slate Metallic		GS-9216	Intense Blue & Olympic Blue	
GS-9212R	Dark Blue Scotchlite & Slate Met.	$267	GS-9216R	Light Blue Scotchlite & Gold Met.	$247
GS-9214	Brown Metallic & Gold Metallic	$327	GS-9217	Light Navy & Slate Metallic	$310
GS-9214R	Brown Metallic & Gold Scotchlite	$215	GS-9217R	Dark Blue Scotchlite & Slate Met.	$267
GS-9215	Light Navy & Bright Blue Metallic	$273	GS-9218	Dark Blue Metallic & Bright Blue Met.	$327
GS-9215R	Dark Blue Scotchlite & Bright Blue Met.	$247	GS-9218R	Dark Blue Scotchlite & Bright Blue Met.	$267
		$308			$327

HOW TO ORDER

1. CALL 612-881-2080 or FAX 612-881-2327. We can help with colors, size or modifications.
2. CAR SPECIFICS: • Make • Year • Model • Color • Number of cars
3. GRAPHIC CHOICE: • Kit number • Reflective or non • Color choice • Unit numbers
Please read the Order Form in our brochure for details on terms, shipping and quantity discounts.

9201 E. BLOOMINGTON FWY., SUITE HH, BLOOMINGTON, MN 55420 • TEL: (612) 881-2080 • FAX (612) 881-2327

grafix shoppe™
CONCEPT TO COMPLETION

2

1. Blending nicely with the curves of this Crown Vic, the yellow and red stripes really set off the dark paint. **2.** Using pre-cut designs and lettering is the easiest method of customizing a police vehicle.

GRAPHICS FOR THE FUTURE

Courtesy of Safariland

1. Safariland, another graphics supplier, envisions future designs as being cleaner and more subdued, though this "stars and stripes" package certainly catches the eye. **2-4.** Industrial Designer Dick Nesbitt, a noted automotive illustrator, proposed these designs for police cars of the future. Note the distinctive lettering used on the car above. While the "Halloween Special" at right is an attractive proposal, it would likely require a custom paint job—an expensive proposition.

GRAPHICS FOR THE FUTURE

1

Courtesy of Grafix Shoppe

2

Courtesy of Grafix Shoppe

1-2. With sport-utility vehicles becoming ever more popular—both for civilian and police use—these computer-generated designs dressing a Jeep Grand Cherokee are certainly relevant for the times. **3.** Try your own hand! Make copies of this drawing and apply your own designs.

3

Courtesy of Grafix Shoppe

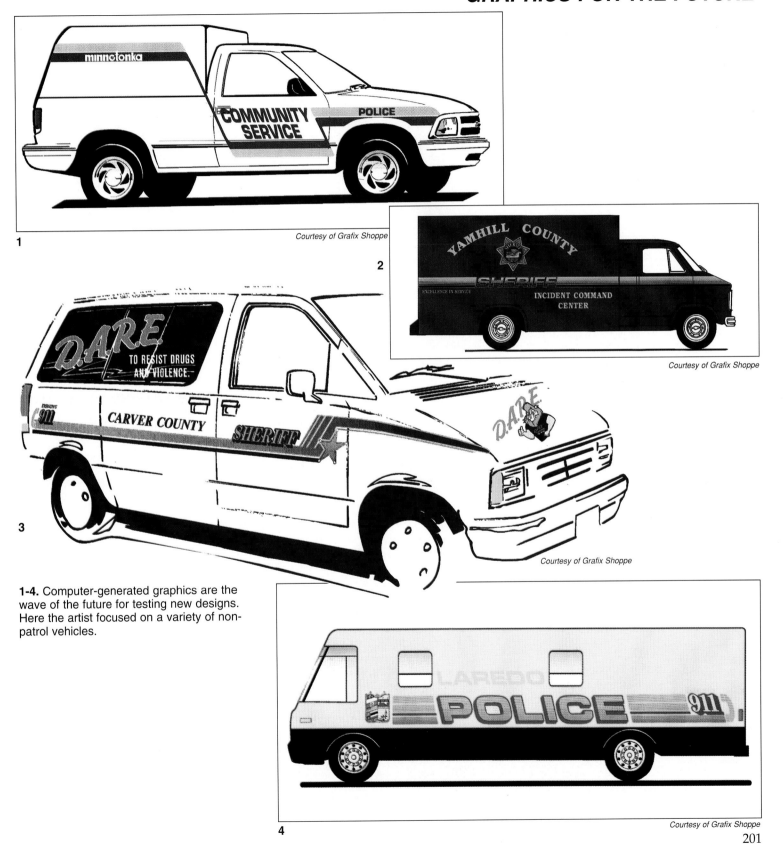

Courtesy of Grafix Shoppe

1-4. Computer-generated graphics are the wave of the future for testing new designs. Here the artist focused on a variety of non-patrol vehicles.

CHAPTER EIGHT

SCALE MODELS AND TOYS

There is an increasing market for police memorabilia, as collectors become aware that there is a very limited supply of such items. Prices are rising as a reflection of this growing scarcity. What started out as a relative handful of ex-law-enforcement officers trading their old department patches or insignias for those of another agency has grown into an international hobby with significant financial involvement. Collectors' items have expanded from only uniform patches to almost any piece of law enforcement gear.

A small but rapidly growing branch of this hobby is the collecting of model and toy law-enforcement vehicles. While most model manufacturers only include an occasional police vehicle in their annual offerings, one company—Road Champs—has stirred things up by introducing an expanded series of quality and inexpensive 1:43 scale late-model cars known to have police packages. This company got the instant attention of collectors when it announced that it intended to produce a model representing every state police agency in the United States. It has also produced models with the markings of some metropolitan and Canadian agencies.

Several manufacturers have issued limited-edition models of law enforcement vehicles that are true collector items due to their accurate design and attention to detail. One such example is an English company called Creaks of Camberly, which produced a series of models depicting antique trucks used by various police constabularies in England. It is doubtful that very many of the 1000 units offered ever left the shores of that country, as they were very much in demand.

Various other makers have produced certain models with exceptional detail—for which they have asked an exceptional price. Corgi, a prominent maker of toy vehicles in England, issued a special limited-edition combined package of a Jaguar MK II and a Morris Mini, both outfitted as English police vehicles, which was widely distributed in the United States.

There are a number of special individual models available from different makers that can be obtained for a stiff price. For example, a distributor of model cars is asking more than $100 for a 1957 De Soto Firesweep wearing Elkhart, Indiana, police trim. A rare 1974 Checker bearing Woodlake police markings and a 1934 Chrysler Airflow two-door in California Highway Patrol trim are available at similar prices. But most collectible model police cars are available for a more reasonable sum if you can find an outlet for them—perhaps a hobby store, or maybe through a special mail-order catalog. Of course, one can always add to a collection at a neighborhood toy store, though few of these will be quality pieces.

True antique models (as opposed to reproductions) are extremely rare—and expensive. Unlike fire-department items, which have always enjoyed a large collector following, there was little interest in police models until fairly recently. As a result, there are few to be found in the typical locations, such as flea markets and antique shops. However, if you do happen upon a true antique police item, you will have a prize that is sure to grow in value.

The ultimate interest in police vehicles is displayed by those who collect actual road-weary patrol cars and turn them into sparkling historic treasures. To support this hobby, there is a Police Car Owners Club with regional chapters spread across the country, which holds an annual meet at a different location each year.

SCALE MODELS AND TOYS

1

2

3

Previous page: 1934 Ford Fordor Sedan. *This page:* **1.** Prior to World War I—before automobiles and trucks became a common part of the economy—boys welcomed cast-iron toys, and police figures were very popular. **2.** This 1:52 scale 1921 Model T Ford van is a good replica of one of the first police vans. By Matchbox, it was made in Macau. **3.** Offered in England, this 1927 Talbot van for the Worchestershire Constabulary of Worchester, England, is from a limited set of collectible police vehicles by Creaks of Camberly and is built on a Matchbox frame. **4.** In the 1980's, the James B. Beam Distilling Co. produced a series of four police-vehicle decanters, and this 1931 Ford police paddy wagon was the second offering.

4

SCALE MODELS AND TOYS

1. This finely detailed 1929 Ford Touring Car was the first of four police-vehicle decanters offered by the James B. Beam Distilling Co. **2.** This accurately detailed Crosley truck of the Hampshire Constabulary was one of the set of four English police vehicles produced by Creaks of Camberly and built on a Matchbox frame. **3.** The Ertl Company produced this 1931 Hawkeye tow truck. This "wrecker," as they used to be called, is an unusual model for a police vehicle. **4.** This 1932 Model B Ford Convertible has many details, such as the glass side-window air deflectors, spotlights, and even a rear license plate holder. The shield on the trunk lid is from the City of Corinth, Mississippi. The model was made by Eligor, in France. **5.** Also by Eligor, and just as nicely detailed, is this 1932 Model B Ford Tudor in 1:43 scale. Many police departments have a Model B in their past.

1

2

3

4

5

205

SCALE MODELS AND TOYS

1

2

3

1. This 1934 Ford Fordor Sedan is the third of four decanters released by the James B. Beam Distilling Co. **2.** Made in France by Rex Toys, this 1935 Ford V-8 Fordor Sedan is in 1:43 scale. **3.** Also made in France, this 1931 Cadillac Sedan in 1:43 scale is by Solido. The star on the door reads "County Police." **4.** Also a product of Rex Toys and made in France is this 1935 Ford Tudor. The markings identify this popular (in its time) police car as being from the State of Montana Highway Patrol. **5.** There is no record of the Indiana State Police putting 1935 Chrysler Airflow cars on patrol, but this 1:43 scale model, made in Portugal by Rex Toys, carries the proper markings.

4

5

1

2

3

4

5

6

7

1. This reproduction of Dick Tracy's police car is a Disney product made in China by Ertl. **2.** This 1:43 scale 1939 Chevrolet Highway Patrol Sedan was made in England by Lledo PLC as part of their Days Gone collection. **3.** This 1937 Chevrolet Delivery Van carries the markings of the Texas Department of Public Safety Highway Patrol. It is actually a heavy bank, made in China and distributed by Spec Cast. **4.** Made in China, this 1:43 Sheriff's 1940 Ford "Woody" Station Wagon is the sixth in a series of vintage autos by Ertl. **5.** During and after World War II, vehicles were hard to obtain, even for police departments, so many used surplus military vehicles like this 1942 Dodge ¾-ton 4×4 utility truck. This one carries the markings for an emergency response unit for the Jeffersonville, Indiana, Police. It is part of the Days Gone collection, made in England by Lledo PLC. **6.** It is doubtful that the South Bend, Indiana, Police Department ever purchased 1948 Chrysler Sedans for its fleet, but that is how this 1:43 model from Solido is marked. It was made in Portugal. **7.** Of course, the military also had police vehicles, and this 1:43 scale 1945 Willys "Jeep" is exceptionally detailed. It was made in Macau by Victoria Cinerius Ltd.

SCALE MODELS AND TOYS

1

2

3

4

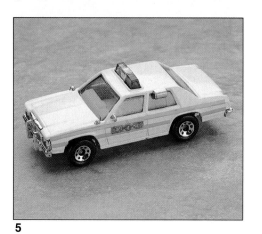

5

6

1. The Danbury Mint imparted their traditional attention to quality to this superbly diecast 1949 Mercury Police Cruiser. Details include a spare tire in the trunk, jacket and nightstick on the front seat, and dashboard-mounted radio speaker. **2.** This 1950 Chevrolet sedan, marked for the South Bend Police, was made in France by Solido. **3.** Volkswagens were popular everywhere, and this 1949 model with Policia markings was made in Portugal by Vitesse. **4.** This 1953 Pontiac Delivery Van carries Detroit Police markings. It was made in England for the Days Gone collection by Lledo PLC. **5.** This 1:69 scale Illinois State Police Chevrolet Impala is by Majorette. **6.** This Morris Minor Saloon, a popular police vehicle in England, was made in China by Corgi.

1

2

1. The Netherlands Police actually used Porsche convertibles, such as this 1952 model, to patrol their highways. But this 1:43 scale version carries Swiss license plates. It was made by Brumm in Italy. 2. There is no record of any police department actually using a BMW Isetta, but this one is marked as being for the German Polizei. It is 1:43 scale and was made in Germany by Schuco. 3. Carrying the familiar markings of the California Highway Patrol, this 1:43 scale 1957 Chevy Bel Air was made in China for Corgi. 4. Conservatively marked, as were most English police vehicles, this 1:43 scale Jaguar MK I was made in France. 5. This Jaguar MK II, made in China for Corgi, is a limited edition for the Durham Constabulary in England.

3

4

5

SCALE MODELS AND TOYS

1. No state highway patrol agency would ever admit to having used a 1962 Corvair Monza for patrol duty, but those are the markings this 1:43 scale unit carries. It was made by Eligor in France. 2. This 1:43 scale Morris Mini, made in China for Corgi, is also a limited edition for the Durham Constabulary in England. 3. This small Ford Bronco, in 1:64 scale, identifies the manufacturer only as Zee. 4. According to Matchbox, the Lindberg City Police Department had a very bright 1979 Plymouth Gran Fury. This 1:36 scale model was made in China. 5. Majorette produced this 1:69 scale Chevrolet Impala in the true colors of the Minnesota Highway Patrol. During this period, the State Trooper identification actually did appear on the front fenders.

1

2

3

4

5

SCALE MODELS AND TOYS

1. This 1990 Chevrolet Caprice with State Trooper markings is the fourth and last in the police-car decanter series from the James B. Beam Distilling Co. **2.** Majorette released this French-made 1:41 scale Chevrolet Impala labeled as a California Highway Patrol vehicle, but the markings were never an official part of that agency's graphics. **3.** This Morris "J" van, with the Tile St. Police Station identification, is listed as a Promotional Model by Lledo PLC.
4. Matchbox offered this Macau-produced 1:69 scale Ford LTD as a 1987 Chicago patrol car. It is even equipped with a radar unit in the back window. **5.** This BMW 528i, in 1:43 scale, was made by GAMA in Germany, but the vehicle identification is not for that country. **6.** This 1:69 scale SWAT Unit vehicle is identified only as a Ford LTD.
7. Matchbox also produced this 1:69 scale Ford LTD in Thailand. It is marked as a Michigan State Police vehicle, but that agency only equips its vehicles with a single rotating light on the top.

1

2

3

4

5

6

7

SCALE MODELS AND TOYS

1

2

3

4

5

1. This 1:69 scale Porsche pursuit vehicle has no manufacturer identification.
2. Yonezawa Toys of Japan made this 1:43 scale Mazda RX-7 with Japanese police markings. 3. This German Polizei van, approximately 1:36 scale, was produced in Germany, but has no manufacturer listed.
4. Matchbox made this 1:69 scale Mercedes-Benz 280 German police unit in Thailand. 5. The Opel Kadett (left) and VW Golf, both in approximately 1:75 scale, were made by an unknown German manufacturer.
6. Matchbox produced this 1:95 scale school bus in China. 7. Road Champs produced this Ohio State Highway Patrol 1992 Chevy Caprice in 1:43 scale.

6

7

1. This Super Kings series 1:43 scale Peterbilt wrecker/tow truck by Matchbox is quite nicely detailed. Die-cast in China, this heavy truck even has movable booms and workable balance outriggers. **2.** Road Champs developed an entire line of 1:43 scale Chevrolet Caprice and Ford Crown Victoria models in various State Police markings. It is their intent to have a complete series of every state law enforcement agency. Shown here is the Rhode Island State Police Ford Crown Victoria. **3.** This is the Road Champs Missouri State Highway Patrol Ford Crown Victoria. **4.** The Road Champs Illinois State Police Chevrolet Caprice is shown with its pre-1996 graphics. **5.** This Road Champs Royal Canadian Mounted Police Chevrolet Caprice carries very modern graphics.

1

2

3

4

5

SCALE MODELS AND TOYS

1

2

3

4

5

6

1. Matchbox produced this German Polizei Mercedes 300E in 1:61 scale. Road Champs has produced a number of models depicting cars of different agencies, among them being (**2**) a Minnesota State Patrol Chevrolet Caprice, (**3**) a South Carolina State Highway Patrol Chevrolet Caprice, (**4**) a New York State Police Chevrolet Caprice, (**5**) a Wisconsin State Patrol Chevrolet Caprice, and (**6**) a Florida Highway Patrol Ford Crown Victoria with Vision lightbar.

INDEX